A Starting-Point Guide

Geneva, Switzerland

And the Lake Geneva Area

Barry Sanders – writing as:

B G Preston

Geneva, Switzerland

ISBN: 9798414447955

1st Edition – April 2022

Acknowledgements: The author greatly appreciates Sandra Sanders' contributions and guidance.

Photography & Maps: Photos and maps in the Starting-Point Guides are a mixture of those by the author and other sources such as Shutterstock, Wikimedia, Google Earth and Google Maps. This edition also includes several photographs which were provided by Geneve.com. No photographs or maps in this work should be used without checking with the author first.

Cover Photo: Courtesy of Geneve.com

~ ~ ~ ~ ~ ~

Table of Contents

Preface: The "Starting-Point" Traveler.. 2

1: Geneva Introduction.. 9

2: Traveling to Geneva.. 22

3: When to Visit 27

4: Where to Stay in Geneva 34

5: Geneva City & Swiss Travel Passes 45

6: Getting Around in Geneva 54

7: Shopping and Local Specialties... 62

8: Museums, Monuments, & Other Attractions 72

9: Lake Geneva Ferries and Towns 91

10: Visiting & Exploring Lausanne 107

11: Annecy Day Trip 115

12: Mont Blanc & Salève Adventures from Geneva 121

Starting-Point Travel Guides.. 129

~ ~ ~ ~ ~ ~

Preface: The "Starting-Point" Traveler
Some General Travel Suggestions

Introduction:

This Starting-Point guide is intended for travelers who wish to really get to know a city and area and not just make it one quick stop on a tour through Switzerland or Europe. Oriented around the concept of using Geneva[1] as a basecamp for several days, this handbook provides guidance on sights both in town and along Lake Geneva with the goal of allowing you to have a comprehensive understanding of this beautiful city and area.

Suggestions on how to utilize this vibrant midsize city as your starting point to discover and explore much of the region and lake area follow.

---

[1] **Names used in this guide**: Geneva is often cited as Genève which is the city's name in French. Lake Geneva is known as Lac Léman in French. For simplicity, the names of "Geneva" and "Lake Geneva" are used in this guide unless the French equivalent is the formal name for a business, location, or attraction.

Area Covered in this Guide:

The focus or "starting-point" of this guide is the Swiss city of Geneva which is situated in western Switzerland in the canton of Geneva (Genève) and the towns and attractions along Lake Geneva. Much of the Lake Geneva region (known in French as Lac Léman) is covered in this guide including the popular city of Lausanne.

Central Geneva with Lake Geneva in the Background

This is not a complete guide to all of western Switzerland and the neighboring regions of France. Such a guide would go beyond the suggested scope of staying in one town such as Geneva and having enjoyable day trips from there.

The area covered here is for the most popular sights which can be reached by train or car in 90 minutes or less each way.

Itinerary Ideas & Suggested Plan:

Suggested Duration: If your travel schedule allows **plan on staying 3 to 5 nights in Geneva**. This is an area with a wonderful variety of sights outside the town. Several days are needed to gain even a moderate understanding of what the region has to offer. If possible, keep a day open toward the end of your visit to tour or revisit areas which you discover during your first days in the area.

A minimum schedule of 3 nights gives you: (a) an afternoon to explore a section of the town on the day you arrive; (b) a full day to explore the sights in Geneva; then (c) a day to explore the mountains or travel across Lake Geneva by ferry to experience one of the nearby towns. Typically, only one day is needed to explore central Geneva, but there are many adventures nearby and having multiple days is advised if your schedule allows for it.

Visit the Tourist Office: Geneva's Tourist Information Office is located near the main ferry terminal along Quai du Mont-Blanc and next to the Pont du Mont-Blanc bridge. This is a good location for visitors as it is close to the heart of town and to the ferry system which is often a great jumping-off point for explorations.

> ### Geneva Tourist Office Website
> www.Geneve.com

The personnel in the offices, many of whom speak English, can provide current information on available tours, transportation, and places to visit. Even if you have done substantial research

prior to your trip, it is likely you will learn of additional opportunities which you had not previously uncovered.

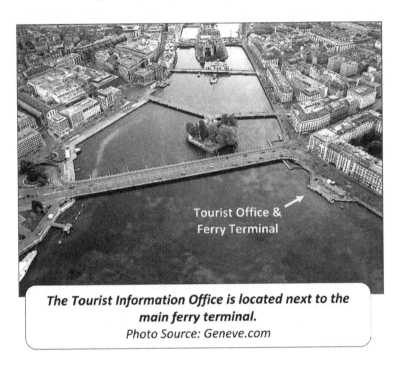

*The Tourist Information Office is located next to the
main ferry terminal.*
Photo Source: Geneve.com

Consider a City Pass: Most cities have discount cards for visitors which can be valuable and reduce hassle if you plan on visiting several attractions. In Geneva, this helpful tool is called the
Geneva City Pass. See Chapter 5 for
details on this card. Available in 24-,
48- and 72-hour variations, this pass
can be a great help and cost saver for
first time visitors.

Obtain information on Local Transportation. Many European cities such as Geneva have excellent tram and bus systems. In the case of Geneva and the lake region, there is a good mix of trams, buses, and ferries which take visitors throughout the city and much of the local area.

Geneva has excellent tram, bus, and ferry networks.
Photo Source: Sdnegel - Wikimedia

Understanding this system can be daunting at first. The staff at the Tourist Office will be able to provide help and transportation maps. See Chapter 6 for details on the area's transportation options and how to use them.

Download some Apps:

With the incredible array of apps for Apple and Android devices, almost every detail you will need for a great trip is available up to and including where to find public toilets.

Geneva Specific apps:

- **Geneva City Guide:** Provided by Switzerland Tourism with details on lodging, dining, and attractions in Geneva.

- **Geneva Travel Guide:** This app is not affiliated with the local travel service. It provides helpful maps for shopping, dining, and leading attractions.

- **TPG / Geneva Tram and Bus Map:** Geneva Public Transport app with bus, tram, and train schedules and routes.

Geneva Travel Guide App

Switzerland Travel and Helpful Information:

- **SBB Trains:** The Swiss national train system. Schedules, routes, and ability to purchase train tickets.

- **Swiss Events:** The app provides updated information on thousands of small and large events throughout the country.

- **PubliBike:** Bicycle rentals are common and fun in Switzerland. This app provides details on all rental locations, bike and e-bike availability, and the ability to rent bikes directly from the app.

- **Switzerland Mobility:** Details on hiking, biking, and cross-country skiing throughout Switzerland including trail details.

- **Swiss Travel Guide:** Similar to the SBB Trains app, but broader in that it includes bus, ferry, and train schedules along with details on key attractions.

- **Swiss Travel Pass:** The perfect app and service to use for travel by almost every mode of transportation in Switzerland. One caution, the pass is expensive.

General Travel Apps:[2]

- **Rome2Rio:** An excellent way to research all travel options including rental cars, trains, flying, ferries, and taxis. The app provides the ability to purchase tickets directly online.

- **Trip Advisor:** Probably the best overall app for finding details on most hotels, restaurants, excursions, and attractions.

- **Flush:** A very helpful app which provides guidance on where to find public toilets.

~ ~ ~ ~ ~ ~

---

[2] **General Travel Apps:** There are dozens of excellent travel apps to select from. The ones cited here are recommended by the author, but your search for helpful apps should not be limited to this.

1: Geneva Introduction

If you were to play a word game with friends and asked them to use one term to describe their image of Geneva, chances are you would hear words such as: sophisticated, worldly, cultured, cosmopolitan, or classy. These terms are accurate as this is a world-class, sophisticated city. It is also a city which fully embraces nature with its beautiful surroundings.

There is something here for everyone ranging from culture to outdoor sports. The presence of many major organizations

View of central Geneva
Photo Source: Geneve.com

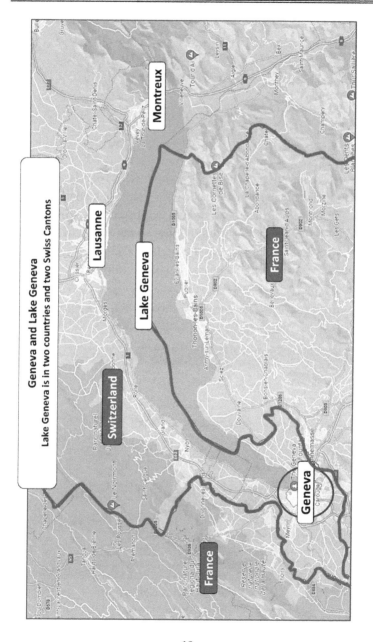

Geneva and Lake Geneva
Lake Geneva is in two countries and two Swiss Cantons

Montreux

Lausanne

Lake Geneva

Switzerland

France

Geneva

France

such as the United Nations and World Health Organization create a truly international flavor. This is Europe's most international city in terms of the population makeup. Over 40% of people living here are from other countries.

Some of the notable organizations located in Geneva:

 WORLD TRADE ORGANIZATION

 United Nations

 World Health Organization

 WORLD METEOROLOGICAL ORGANIZATION

 International Telecommunication Union

 United Nations Human Rights

OFFICE OF THE HIGH COMMISSIONER FOR HUMAN RIGHTS

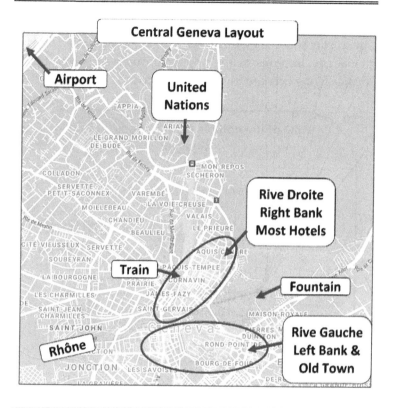

Some Basic Facts about Geneva:

- It is the second largest city in Switzerland with a population of 204,000 in the city proper and 627,000 in the Swiss portions of the metro area. The largest city is Zurich with a population roughly twice of Geneva's.

- The city size is compact making it easy to explore. The total area is only 6 square miles.

- Geneva hosts more international organizations than any other city in the world.

- The currency used here is the Swiss Franc although Euros are in common use. (Note – there is often a surcharge for using Euros). The value of a Swiss Franc (CHF) is roughly 95% of a Euro.

- Lake Geneva (Lac Léman) is the largest lake in central Europe. The lake is shared between France and Switzerland with 60% of the lake area belonging to Switzerland. (See map on page 9).

- The official language is French but, given the international nature of Geneva, English is used by about 25% of residents here.

- This is an expensive city with a high cost of living. Some resources cite Geneva as having the 2nd highest cost of living in Europe with only Zurich ranking slightly higher. Different sources provide differing rankings.

There are many outdoor dining areas such as Place du Molard in the Old Town area.
Photo Source: Geneve.com

What to Expect When Visiting Here:

This is an active and very diverse city. With the presence of many world-renowned organizations, there is naturally a multicultural feel. You can encounter people and hear languages from any part of the globe. There is also a very youthful vibe here due, in part, to several universities such as the University of Geneva with 17,000 students.

The city is surrounded by nature and also by France. The most obvious natural formation is the crescent shaped Lake Geneva which stretches for 45 miles and covers an area of 224 square miles. Nature doesn't stop with the lake. When coming here, visitors soon realize that the city is bordered by mountains such as Mont-Blanc. Mont Salève is only 4 miles from the city center and provides an easy adventure by gondola. Chapter 12 provides details on area mountain adventures. These snow-

Geneva's Right Bank with the Jura Mountains dominating the view.
Photo Source: Geneve.com

capped treasures, although mostly in France, provide a delight-ful backdrop for Geneva.

Geneva is a town of neighborhoods each with their own char-acter. Where you are in town can give a very different feel and set of experiences. The presence of two rivers, the Rhône and the Arve, largely define the areas in town. Most references to the sections and neighborhoods in town will fall into two very broad groupings:

The Right Bank or "Rive Droite:" This is the section of Geneva on the north side of the Rhône and the portion of the lake bor-dered by the city. It is where many leading hotels, the main train station, and the main ferry terminal are located. It is also an area

The UN complex is on the right bank area of Geneva.
Photo Source: Geneve.com

with numerous bars and nightclubs. There is even a noted red-light district here, not far from the train station. The United Nations facilities are located at the northern part of the Right Bank.

Specific neighborhood names cited for this gen-eral area include Les Paquis, Saint-Gervais, Mont-Blanc, and the Na-tions area.

The Left Bank or "Rive Gauche:" The large area to the south of the lake and the Rhône. It also includes the Arve River and the

**The Jet D'Eau on Geneva's
left bank.**
Photo Source: Geneve.com

junction of the two rivers. The famous Geneva fountain, Jet d'Eau, is here along with the Old Town/City Center section.[3]

Most of the major museums and some of the more noted shopping districts are here. The large University of Geneva is here along with outdoor markets and major plazas such as the Plaine de Plainpalais.

Neighborhood names such as Rue-Basses, Carouge, Plainpalais, and Eaux-Vives are included in this area of town.

Many visitors will find that this side of the river is where most of their city explorations will occur, even if they are staying on the right bank.

---

[3] **Old Town vs City Center:** Usage of these terms can be a little confusing as they are often used interchangeably and the two do overlap. Old Town is the historical and oldest area of Geneva which sits slightly south of the river and much of it is uphill while the City Center section is near the lake in the area known as Eaux-Vives. This guide will generally use the "Old Town" term to encompass this combined area.

Caution: The true historic Old Town section is hilly with many narrow and steep roads. This can be problematic for individuals with mobility limitations.

Shopping in Geneva:

Watches, chocolate, cheese, perfumes, and fine apparel. Geneva has it all and it is a shopping destination city for individuals from all over the globe. To add to this, it can be a very upscale and pricey shopping experience, but not always.

> **Plan Around Closings:**
>
> To ensure your time in Geneva is not wasted, it is important to note the following:
>
> Most shops are closed on Sunday.
>
> Many museums are closed on Monday.

At the very least, there is some great window shopping to do along impressive boulevards. Many major brands of clothing, cosmetics, and jewelry have stores here. Head to the central shopping areas of Rue du Rhône on the left bank or Rue du Mont-Blanc on the right bank. Both areas feature notable shopping and outlets for labels such as: Anne Fontaine, Céline, Dior, Armani, and many others.

Shopping is not limited to upscale specialty boutiques. Several major department stores may be found on both sides of the river with the more noted stores such as Globus or Manor. The app, **Geneva Travel Guide,** is a helpful tool to enable you to find the type of shopping you are seeking in and around Geneva.

Geneva is a chocolate lovers paradise and why not do it while wearing one of the world's best watches. When it comes to watches, you can go directly to the watch factories or salons of leading brands such as Patek Philippe or Gubelin or, for something more affordable, visit Swatch.

Geneva Dining and Cuisine:

With over 1,000 restaurants in the Geneva metro area, it soon becomes obvious that this city enjoys dining out. Other aspects of dining in Geneva also quickly become apparent: it can be very expensive; there is a strong French influence; and there is also a multi-cultural influence.

Geneva's food experiences are not limited to restaurants. There are several open markets here which allow you to select fresh local specialties for a great lunch or dinner back at your lodging. One of the largest markets is on Boulevard Helvétique near the city's Old Town and conveniently located next to the impressive art and history museum.

Several restaurants such as the Edelweiss in the Pâquis-Centre section of town specialize in fondue dining.
Photo Source: Geneve.com

This array of dining experiences is one reason for having a city app on your cellphone. Also, chapter 7 in this guide provides listings of some of the popular outdoor markets and fondue restaurants.

Some History:

Recorded history for Geneva goes back to the early Roman Empire. This had been an early border town and fort to guard against the Celtic tribes known as Helvetians. Later, in the Middle Ages, Geneva (often cited as Genevois), was under the control of the Holy Roman Empire.

1858 Artist's Rendering of Geneva
Photo Source: Wikimedia by National Library of Wales

As happened in much of Europe, various religious movements altered who was in control and, in turn, the primary religion and even the architecture shifted. Calvinism, a part of the

Protestant Reformation started in Geneva in the 16th century. Around this time, the Republic of Geneva was established, and it aligned itself with the Swiss Confederacy.

France, with its predominantly Catholic religion, took over in the 18th century and remained under France's control until the end of the Napoleonic Wars in 1814. From that time until today, the Canton of Geneva has been fully aligned with the Swiss Confederation.

Lake Geneva:

If your time in Geneva allows, get out and explore some of the towns and sights along Lake Geneva. It is easy to do and you have several enjoyable options ranging from train trips, to guided tours, to catching one of the many ferries.

View of Lake Geneva from a hillside vineyard with a ferry traveling by.
Photo Source: Wikimedia - By Severin.Stalder

There are three sectors of the lake and use of these terms help define the part of the lake a town is on:

- Petit Lac: The western area of Lake Geneva. It is the narrowest stretch and is generally shallower than other sections. This is where Geneva is.

- Grand Lac: The largest section of the lake which covers most of the eastern area. The city of Lausanne is here.

- Haut Lac: The smallest in size, near the point where the Rhône enters the lake. The town of Montreux is here.

Much of the lakeside is populated, providing many towns and villages to explore. This can be a lot of fun, especially if you take a ferry. Many of these destinations, both in Switzerland and France, have convenient ferry terminals and something to offer the visitor. These towns often are great jumping off spots for day hikes.

The largest town is Lausanne with a population of 130,000. It is a beautiful destination and best reached by train. Other towns such as Yvoire in France or Montreux in Switzerland can be reached by ferry, train, or car and are well worth the trip.

You also have options of simply going out on a short lake cruise, often with a helpful narrative of the sights you are seeing. The easiest way to travel the Geneva harbor area of the lake is to take one of the colorful water taxis. A good place to catch one is at the ferry terminal on the right bank.

Chapter 9 provides more information on using the local ferry and train systems and chapters 9 & 10 outline the sights in several of the more popular towns.

~ ~ ~ ~ ~ ~

2: Traveling to Geneva

Geneva is a major destination, so it is generally easy to find convenient travel to this city by almost any mode of travel.

The airport, train, and bus stations are all very close to the heart of town. They are connected to each other and to the heart of town by trams and buses.

Geneva'a airport, train, and bus stations are close to downtown.

Arriving by Train:

The main train station, Gare Cornavin (also known as Gare de Genève), is close to the center of town and to the airport. If you have booked lodging on the right bank, you might be able to walk to your hotel. Walking time from the station to most right-bank hotels will be under 10 minutes.[4]

One caution. This is a big, busy, and multi-level station with many shops and restaurants plus different departure areas. Pay close attention to signs when you are striving to navigate through the Geneva train station as it is easy to get confused.

The tram and local bus system services this busy station and there is a tram stop directly outside of the station. Chapter 6 provides details on the local transportation system.

Gare de Genève / Gare Cornavin - Geneva's main train station is only a few blocks from the lakeshore.
Photo Source: Google Earth

---

[4] **More than 1 Train Station**: Gare Cornavin is, by far, the busiest in Geneva, but some local trains depart from the Eaux-Vives station which is across town on the other side of the river and lake.

If you are needing to make a train-to-airport connection, this is easy to do. There is a direct tram link between the two facilities with a travel time of only 6 minutes.

Example Train Travel Times to/from Geneva		
From	**Avg Travel Time**	**Trains Per Day**
Bern, Switzerland	1 hr 45 min	20+
Lyon, France	2 hr	10+
Marseille, France	4 hr	5 to 10
Milan, Italy	4 hr 30 min	5 to 10
Paris, France	3 hr 30 min	5 to 10
Zurich, Switzerland	2 hr 45 min	10+

A great travel site to consider:	When making your travel plans for travel by train, check out Rome2rio.com. This site provides and compares travel time and costs for train, driving, and bus.
Rome2rio	

Flying to Geneva:

The Geneva airport, GVA, is very active. It has the curious element of having much of its northern edge located immediately on the French border. It is also very close to the heart of Geneva so, for most destinations around the city, minimal ground-travel time will be required.

Many different airlines fly directly into here with departures to and from major cities throughout Europe, Africa, the Mid East, and North America. Once you arrive, there are numerous options for travel into town.

Trams: Geneva's tram lines connect to the airport with a rail stop on the lower level. Full maps of this system are posted to help guide you. Not all areas of central Geneva are convenient to the trams so, in some cases, you may find that a bus or taxi will be better. Upon arriving, collect a pass which allows you to travel free for a limited period.

Taxi and Limousine: This mode of travel is something of a mixed blessing. On the downside, travel by either limo or taxi in the Geneva area can be expensive. Expect to pay a minimum of 40 CHF (around $45 or 38€) plus tip to reach most central Geneva

> **Free Bus and Tram Ticket**
> Fun fact… when you fly into Geneva, you may pick up a free ticket which is valid for 80 minutes on local transportation. There is a ticket machine in baggage claim to obtain these passes.

locations. On the positive side, the convenience of being taken directly to your lodging or other in-town destination can be a great stress reliever.

Taxis are readily available at the departures area, so reservations are not needed. Limos generally should be reserved in advance. Two services, among many, include: **GenevaAirportTransfer.net** and **GMC-Limousines.com.**

~ ~ ~ ~ ~ ~

3: When to Visit

Your best times to visit western Switzerland vary largely by your goals and activities. Geneva, along with much of Switzerland, is a popular tourist destination. It is, even around Geneva, a noted destination for outdoor sports such as hiking or winter skiing. Put another way, you are rarely crowd-free here.

These differing elements lead to a situation where there is not a true off season. If you are seeking a mixture of only moderate crowding along with the ability to enjoy the lake area and surrounding country, consider coming in one of the two shoulder seasons of: Spring, mid-April to early June, or Fall, late September to November.

Geneva and Switzerland are expensive to visit, and the costs naturally ramp up in the peak summer and winter seasons. Coming in one of the shoulder-seasons can reduce your travel costs. In the winter, skiers find Geneva a good basecamp to explore the miles of cross-country ski trails or several nearby downhill ski areas. In the summer months, the endless array of mountain trails and boating activities are popular draws.

Some Seasonal Considerations:

Fall: Not as crowded as other times of the year. Rains are frequent in late fall. Temperatures are generally cool. Several tourist activities and attractions will close or have reduced hours curing this time of year.

Winter: Crowds pick up for winter festivals and winter activities, especially skiing. Prices are greater than the fall. Temperatures are cold, but not horribly so, unless you head up into the mountains. Late January to mid-February are generally the coldest periods, but the average temperatures are not much below freezing. One caution, the winds from the lake can bring a noted windchill.

You don't have to go far to enjoy winter sports in Geneva.
Photo Source: Geneve.com

Spring: The other of the two shoulder seasons which gives visitors the ability to still get in some skiing in the higher elevations or explore the lake area in cool temperatures. Some resorts will be closed during this time of year. Rain is common so dress accordingly.

Summer: The busiest and most expensive time of the year. There are many pluses to visiting here during July and August. Hiking in the mountains or boat trips on Lake Geneva are top among the positives for visiting Geneva in the summer. The climate is typically mild and, even at the height of summer, not overly hot or humid.

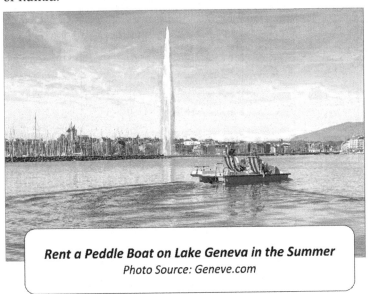

Rent a Peddle Boat on Lake Geneva in the Summer
Photo Source: Geneve.com

Typical Climate by Month:

Average Geneva Climate by Month [5]			
Month		**Avg High**	**Avg Low**	**Avg Rain**
Jan	☹	41 F / 5 C	30 F / - 1 C	2.9 inches

[5] **Climate Data Source:** Wikipedia.com

Average Geneva Climate by Month [5]				
Month		**Avg High**	**Avg Low**	**Avg Rain**
Feb	☹	45 F / 7 C	30 F / -1 C	2.2 inches
Mar	😐	53 F / 12 C	35 F / 2 C	2.4 inches
Apr	😐	61 F / 16 C	41 F / 5 C	2.6 inches
May	☺	68 F / 20 C	48 F / 9 C	3.1 inches
Jun	☺	76 F / 24 C	55 F / 13 C	3.3 inches
Jul	😐	80 F / 27 C	58 F / 15 C	3.1 inches
Aug	😐	79 F / 26 C	58 F / 14 C	3.2 inches
Sep	☺	70 F / 21 C	51 F / 11 C	3.6 inches
Oct	☺	60 F / 16 C	45 F / 7 C	3.8 inches
Nov	😐	49 F / 9 C	37 F / 3 C	3.5 inches
Dec	☹	42 F / 6 C	32 F / 0 C	3.5 inches

Major Festivals and Events in Geneva:[6]

There are several popular events in and near Geneva each year. Visiting one of these can be a great addition to a tour of the area. The only moderate downsides are the added crowds and increased lodging rates. Information on some of the leading events follow. The website **www.Geneve.com** provides a comprehensive calendar of hundreds of events, concerts, and festivals around the city area and area.

This is not a complete list of all events in and near Geneva. The events listed are some of the more popular ones which have broad appeal. With so many major international organizations located here, there will almost always be an event relating to one of them happening in town.

Winter:

- **Fête de L'Escalade**: Geneva: One of the area's most popular events which occurs in mid-December. The historical background is a celebration of Swiss victory over the Duke of Savoy in 1602. Today, there are parades, musical events, and even races going on. Many food and crafts booths can be found. The focal point of activity is in Geneva's Old Town. The highlight of this festival is a torchlight parade in the evening.

---

[6] **COVID & Omicron impact on events**. Due to the varying and evolving restrictions occurring as a result of the ongoing health crisis, the schedules for many events are negatively impacted. Check the website for each program when making travel plans.

- **Christmas Festival & International Christmas Market**: The focal point of Geneva's Christmas festival (Marchë de Noël) is in Old Town at multiple locations including Fusterie Square and Jardin Anglais (English Garden) adjacent to the lake. It occurs each year from mid-November to the day after Christmas. Numerous crafts and food booths may be found here with many serving local fondue specialties. For children, there is are a carousel and pony rides.

  Full details on this fun set of events may be found at: Noel-Au-Jardin.ch.

- **Geneva International Motor Show**: If you enjoy fine cars this is the place to be. The event is huge and the 2023 "GIMS" will be the 90th in its history. (The 2022 event was canceled due to COVID).

  This is a "don't miss" event. It is held in late February or early March at the Palexpo convention center next to the airport. Full details for upcoming "GIMS" may be found on the website at: www.GIMS.Swiss.

Spring/Summer:

- **Geneva Music Festival** (Fête de la Musique): Across the city, at dozens of venues, are musical groups and acts. Most forms of popular music may be found here, creating a lively atmosphere. This event lasts for two weeks in late May and early June. Tickets are required for several of the shows.

Check www.GenevaMusicalFestival.com for full details and ticket purchases.

- **Geneva Festival:** During August, along the shores of Lake Geneva, is a 10-day open-air celebration of the season, the "Fêtes de Genève." There are numerous music performances, a fair, and parades. The event culminates with fireworks over the lake.

  Important Note: This festival was cancelled in 2021 due to COVID. It is uncertain as of this writing when it will return.

  Details on this city-wide festival may be found at www.FetesDeGeneve.ch.

Fireworks over the lake during the Geneva Festival in August.
Photo Source: Geneve.com

~ ~ ~ ~ ~ ~ ~

4: Where to Stay in Geneva

Where you choose to stay when visiting a new city is essentially a personal choice. You may prefer hotels or rental apartments. Picking a place guided by your budget may be critical to you also.

Regardless of the motives which drive your selection of accommodation type, the "where in town should I stay?" question is critical to helping you have an enjoyable visit.

Budget and accommodation-type issues aside, the following criteria may be of importance to you:

- Convenience to historical sites, restaurants, shopping.
- Convenience to transportation.
- Noise levels around where you will stay.

This guide does not provide details on all hotels in Geneva. There are simply too many to describe, and there are many areas to consider. There are many fine and dynamic online sources such as **Booking.com** or **Trip Advisor** which give far more detail than can be provided here. These sites will provide answers to every question about a property you are considering and allow you to make reservations once you have made your

> **Free Local Transportation**
>
> Most Geneva hotels will provide passes for free local transportation on buses and trams.

selection. Another great resource is the Genève tourist center website. Geneve.com.

When looking at the array of lodging packed into central Geneva, you would be hard-pressed to think of another city with so many top-tier hotels in close proximity. Strolling along the lakefront you will see names such as Ritz-Carlton, Fairmont Grand, and the Four Seasons along with many other world-renowned properties. Step back from the lakefront or over the bridge to the city center/old town sections and the lodging becomes more affordable. Still, regardless of the class of hotel you select, this is an expensive area, so expect to pay more than you would outside of Switzerland.

Several luxury hotels are located on the Lake's Right Bank
Source: Google Earth

Recommended Area:

For first-time visitors whose goal is to explore Geneva and the surrounding area, there are **three suggested areas** to consider. Other sections of town with quality lodging, such as near the airport or the United Nations, are not included in this list simply because they are not as convenient to transportation and the most popular attractions.

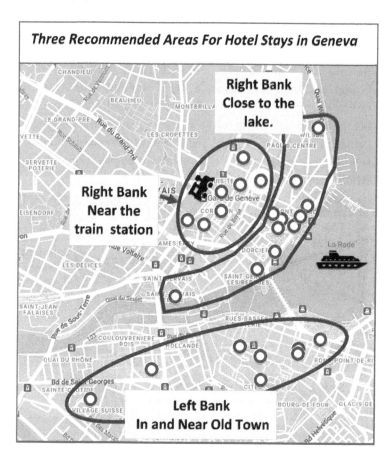

Three Recommended Areas For Hotel Stays in Geneva

Right Bank Close to the lake.

Right Bank Near the train station

Left Bank In and Near Old Town

Lodging of all categories of hotels, inns, B & B and Air B&B type of accommodations may be found here in every section of town. This guide focuses on hotels and inns only.

The three suggested areas for lodging are:

1. Right Bank – along, or close to, the lake shore.

2. Right Bank – near the train station.

3. Left Bank – in the vicinity of the historic Old Town.

Hotels on or near Lake Geneva – Right Bank

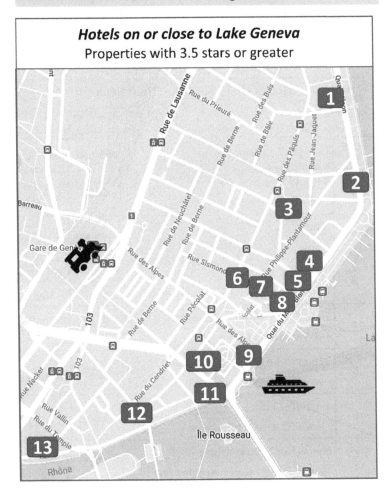

Hotels on or close to Lake Geneva
Properties with 3.5 stars or greater

Along the right bank of the river and lakeshore are numerous hotels, many of which cater to the wealthy. Not all properties here are expensive especially if you step back from the lake a short distance.

There are many advantages to staying here including immediate access to the ferry dock and numerous shops and restaurants. Most of the hotels here are within walking distance of the train station and are also a short walk across the bridge to the Old Town area.

Hotels On or Near the Right Bank			
User ratings of 3.5 stars or greater are a blending of popular sources including: Booking.com, Hotels.com & Trip Advisor.			
Map ID	Hotel Name	Budget	Rating
1	Hotel President Wilson www.Marriott.com	$$$$	5 stars
2	The Woodward www.OetkerCollection.com	$$$$	5 stars
3	Hôtel Edelweiss www.HotelEdelweissGeneva.com	$$	3.5 star
4	Fairmont Grand Hotel Geneva www.Fairmont.com	$$$$	5 stars
5	Hotel d'Angleterre Geneva www.DAngleterreHotel.com	$$$$	5 stars
6	Eastwest Hôtel www.EastwestHotel.ch	$$$	4 stars
7	Swiss Luxury Apartments www.Swiss-Luxury-Apartments.ch	$$$	4.5 stars

Hotels On or Near the Right Bank

User ratings of 3.5 stars or greater are a blending of popular
sources including: Booking.com, Hotels.com & Trip Advisor.

Map ID	Hotel Name	Budget	Rating
8	Beau-Rivage Genève www.Beau-Rivage.ch	$$$$	5 stars
9	The Ritz Carlton de la Paix, Geneva www.RitzCarlton.com	$$$$	5 stars
10	Hôtel Bristol Genève www.Bristol.ch	$$$	4 stars
11	Four Seasons Geneva www.FourSeasons.com	$$$$	5 stars
12	The Ambassador www.The-Ambassador.ch	$$$	4 stars
13	Mandarin Oriental Geneva www.MandarinOriental.com	$$$$	5 stars

Lodging Near the Train Station:

Numerous small and mid-size hotels may be found near Geneva's main train station, "Gare Cornavin." The nature of this area is substantially different from the sector of town along the lake even though it is just a few blocks away. This neighborhood caters more to day-to-day shopping and dining and does not focus on wealthy visitors.

Most of the hotels here could be thought of as "boutique" and are generally in the 3-to-4-star range. Pricing for lodging here is dramatically less than the lakeshore area which is just a couple of blocks away.

A great positive to the Cornavin area is the proximity to the train station. This can be a significant advantage if you will be taking multiple daytrips via train. Also, the walking distance to the lakeshore is under ten minutes for most of these hotels. Many small restaurants and shops are in this area.

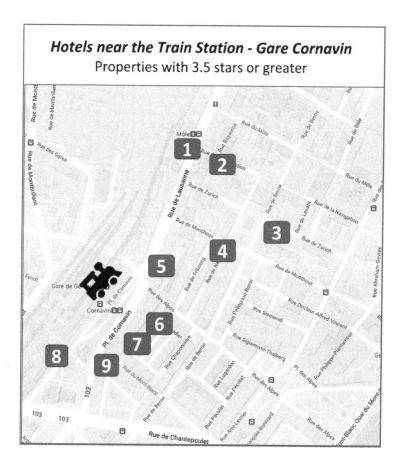

Hotels near the Train Station - Gare Cornavin
Properties with 3.5 stars or greater

One caution, this area is also Geneva's red-light district which is a busy center for exuberant bars and other forms of entertainment.

	Hotels Near the Train Station		
	User ratings of 3.5 stars or greater are a blending of popular sources including: Booking.com, Hotels.com & Trip Advisor.		
Map ID	Hotel Name	Budget	Rating
1	Hotel Auteuil Manotel www.HotelAuteuilGeneva.com	$$$	4 stars
2	Hôtel Kipling Manotel www.HotelKiplingGeneva.com	$$$	3.5 stars
3	Novatel Genève Centre www.All.Accor.com – then search for Geneva.	$$$	3.5 star
4	Hotel D Geneva www.Hotel-Geneva.ch	$$$	4 stars
5	Warwick Geneva www.WarwickHotels.com	$$$	4 stars
6	Hôtel Strasbourg www.FassbindHotels.ch	$$	3.5 stars
7	Hôtel Cristal Design www.FassbindHotels.ch	$$	3.5 stars
8	Hôtel Cornavin www.FassbindHotels.ch	$$	3.5 stars
9	Hôtel Suisse www.Hotel-Suisse.ch	$	3.5 stars

Lodging In Old Town/City Center – Left Bank:

Geneva's Old Town is one of the largest in Europe and is where many museums, parksc and attractions can be found. Staying here provides a good mix of boutique and luxury lodging with moderate to high nightly rates.

The area is a pleasant maze of narrow roads with numerous plazas and many hotels are right in the center of nearly 2,000 years of history.

The biggest negative to staying here is distance to transportation. For many, that is minor when looking at the plus of having a vast array of local cafes, restaurants, and shops so close by. This area is also where the large University of Geneva is located, which adds to a youthful and active vibe.

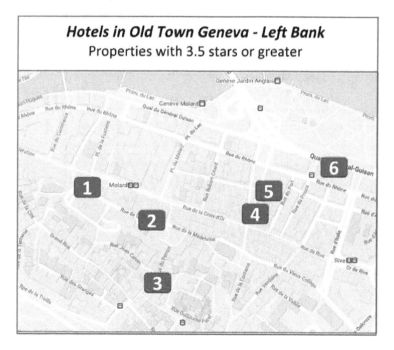

Hotels in Old Town Geneva - Left Bank
Properties with 3.5 stars or greater

Hotels in Old Town & City Center Geneva – Left Bank

User ratings of 3.5 stars or greater are a blending of popular sources including: Booking.com, Hotels.com & Trip Advisor.

Map ID	Hotel Name	Budget	Rating
1	Fraser Suites Geneva www.FraserHospitality.com	$$$$	4 stars
2	citizenM Geneva www.CitizenM.com	$$$	4.5 stars
3	Hôtel Les Armures www.LesArmures.ch	$$$$	4.5 star
4	Hôtel de la Cigogne www.LongeMalleCollection.com	$$$$	4.5 stars
5	Hôtel Longemalle Genève www.LongmalleCollection.com	$$$$	4 stars
6	Hôtel Métropole Genève www.Metroplle.ch	$$$$	4.5 stars

Staying in other towns on Lake Geneva:

Chapter 9 provides an overview of several charming lakeside towns. Several of these locales provide delightful stays with wonderful scenery and opportunities to explore area mountains, lakeside castles, and even vineyards.

If your travel schedule allows, consider splitting your stay in the Lake Geneva area by having a few nights in Geneva and at least one night in one of the following towns along the eastern edges of Lake Geneva. This is not a comprehensive list as there are many wonderful areas to consider staying in.

- Lausanne, Switzerland: A charming and vibrant city of nearly 140,000 people. Easy to reach by train or ferry. (See chapter 10 on Lausanne for details).

- Montreux, Switzerland: In the heart of the area known as "The Swiss Riviera." A beautiful small city with easy mountain access.

- Evian-les-Bains, France: An upscale spa town across the lake from Lausanne and Montreux.

View of the lake and mountains from the Grand Hotel Suisse in Montreux
Source: Wikimedia Commons

~ ~ ~ ~ ~ ~

5: Geneva City & Swiss Travel Passes

A Convenient Way to Discover the City & Area

If you will be staying in Geneva for several days and wish to visit multiple attractions, then acquiring the Geneva City Pass can be a good idea. This pass is also referred to as "Geneva Live" on some sites. Another option, which focuses on transportation, is the Swiss Travel Pass. This country-wide pass is described further in this chapter. Do not buy both.

Geneva, like most cities in Europe, offers city passes that provide discounted or free admissions to many attractions. In Geneva, the pass includes access to fifty+ museums, tours, and notable sites. It also includes **free use of the local transportation** system which can be a huge advantage if you are likely to use local buses, ferries, or trams.

Full details on this pass and what it covers may be found at www.Geneve.com.

Some of the attractions listed in the pass are free such as many of the museums. Also, if you are staying in a local hotel, it is likely they will provide a voucher for free travel during the duration of your stay. Still, even with this, the benefits provided by the passes are often worth it.

In General, the Passes Include:

- Free or discounted admission to numerous museums and attractions.
- Free use of local transportation.
- Discounts to many tours.
- Discounts at numerous local shops and restaurants.
- Discounts on bicycle and paddle boat rentals.

Pass Options Available and Pass Pricing:

The **Geneva City Pass** is available in three different durations of: 24, 48, and 72 hours. In each case, the pass's time frame starts with its first use. The array of attractions included in the pass is the same, regardless of the duration.

One note of caution: when purchasing a pass from the website, you are required to indicate the starting date for the pass. If you are uncertain when you will start to use it, it may be best to wait and purchase the city pass from the tourist office

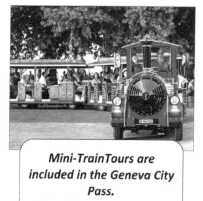

Mini-TrainTours are included in the Geneva City Pass.
Photo Source: Geneve.com

which is centrally located near the main ferry dock on the right bank. If you purchase a city pass from the Geneva Tourist Office, they will provide you with a free detailed map of the area at that time.

When you use the city pass for local attractions or discounts with area merchants, the pass may be used only once per person.

Where to Purchase:

- In town: at the tourist office and some hotels also sell these passes.
- Online: Geneve.com and numerous resellers such as: Viator.com and GetYourGuide.com.

Geneva City Pass Pricing: [7]				
Online pricing. Fares may be slightly more when purchased directly from the Tourist Office or third-party sources				
Duration	**Adult Rate**	**Amount in Other Currencies** (Approximate)		
		Euro	**USD**	**Pound**
24-Hour	26 CHF	25€	$28	£21
48-Hour	37 CHF (18,50 per day)	36€	$40	£30
72-Hour	45 CHF (15,00 per day)	44€	$49	£36,50

[7] **Price Note:** Pricing cited here is from March, 2022 and is subject to change. Check with **Geneve.com** or the Tourist Office while in Geneva for current pass cost. Currency conversions can and do change so use the costs shown here as a rough estimate only.

What is Included in the Geneva City Pass:

Some of What the Geneva City Pass Includes		
Category	**Attraction**	**Free or Discount**
Transportation & Tours	City Trams and Buses	Free
	Carouge Walking Tour	Discount
	Chocolate Tour Walking tour of Swiss Chocolate factories and stores.	Discount
	Geneva International Tour on Trolley Bus	Free
	Mini-Train Tours	Free
	Rhône River Cruise	Discount
	Taxi Bike Tour	Discount
	Geneva Sunset Tour	Discount
	Cruise Tour of the sights of Geneva from a boat	Free
Museums	Archaeological Site of St. Peters' Cathedral	Free
	Ariana Museum A museum devoted to ceramics and glass.	Free

Some of What the Geneva City Pass Includes		
Category	**Attraction**	**Free or Discount**
Museums	Barbier-Mueller Museum Africa, Asia, and Oceania art museum	Free
	Baur foundation Museum of Far Eastern Art	Free
	Centre d'Art Contemporain Contemporary Art Museum	Free
	Château de Voltaire The 18th century home of philosopher Voltaire.	Free
	Ethnography Museum Museum of world cultures	Free
	Musée d'art et d'Histoire Art and history museum	Free
	Natural History Museum	Free
	Patek Philippe Museum Watchmaking history museum.	Free
	Prangins Château & Swiss National Museum	Free
	Red Cross International Museum	Free

Some of What the Geneva City Pass Includes		
Category	**Attraction**	**Free or Discount**
Mountain Explorations	Mount Salève Cable Car	Free
	Chamonix & Mont Blanc Day Trip	Discount
	Montreaux Glacier and Mountain Tour	Discount
Sporting Activities and Rentals	Boat Rental Rent a motorboat or paddle boat on Lake Geneva.	Discount
	Canoes on the Rhône Rent a canoe to explore the Rhône River	Discount
	Stand Up Paddle Board Rental on Lake Geneva	Free
	Geneva Beach Beach Waterpark	Free
	Canoeing on the Arve River	Discount

~ ~ ~ ~ ~ ~

Swiss Travel Pass (Previously called the "Swiss Pass") [8]

This popular travel pass allows you to use most of Switzerland's transportation system including trains, bus, and ferry systems, and many mountain lifts and gondolas.

> **The Swiss Travel Pass is expensive.**
>
> Only acquire one if you plan on being in Switzerland for at least 3 days and plan on taking multiple journeys each day.

When using this pass, separate reservations are not needed for train tickets, so this adds a significant savings in travel planning.

This pass also includes many museums, eliminating the need to purchase the Geneva City Pass. With the Swiss Travel Pass you may take an unlimited number of trips on included modes of transportation.

What it covers:

> Children travel free when they are with an adult who has a Swiss Travel Pass.

- All of Switzerland
- Unlimited train travel
- Unlimited ferry travel
- Unlimited bus travel
- Free or discounted travel on select mountain rail and gondolas.
- 500+ museums, free entry.

Variations: A complex array of pass options are available.

- Class: Purchase passes for 1st or 2nd class travel.

---

[8] **Swiss Travel Pass vs the Swiss Pass:** The "Swiss Pass" is intended to be used only by Swiss residents. Visitors should consider the "Swiss Travel Pass."

- Days Covered: purchase passes for 3, 4, 6, 8, or 15 days.

- Flex or standard days: Ticket options cover # of days as a group or flex.

  o Non-Flex: The # of days covered are in sequence.

  o Flex, the days purchased, such as 4 days, must be used within 1 month of purchase, but do not need to be used in sequence. This variation is more expensive.

- Age of Traveler: Two price tiers are available: Adults and "Youth" for individuals between 16-24 years old. The youth ticket's cost is roughly 70% of the adult rate.

Cost: Given the many variables, it is best to check the Travel Pass website to determine the cost of a pass which best fits your needs. Some price examples follow.

Swiss Travel Pass Price Examples				
Adult Rates and Currency Conversions are as of Spring 2022 – subject to change. CHF = Swiss Franc				
Days Covered	Standard		Flex Days	
	2nd Class	1st Class	2nd Class	1st Class
3 Days	232 CHF $249 226€ £189	369 CHF $396 360€ £301	267 CHF $287 261€ £218	424 CHF $455 414€ £346
4 Days	281 CHF $302 274€ £229	447 CHF $480 436€ £365	323 CHF $347 315€ £264	514 CHF $552 502€ £419

Swiss Travel Pass Price Examples				
Adult Rates and Currency Conversions are as of Spring 2022 – subject to change. CHF = Swiss Franc				
Days Covered	**Standard**		**Flex Days**	
	2nd Class	**1st Class**	**2nd Class**	**1st Class**
8 Days	389 CHF $418 380€ £317	617 CHF $663 602€ £504	409 CHF $439 399€ £334	649 CHF $697 633€ £530
15 Days	429 CHF $461 419€ £350	675 CHF $725 659€ £551	449 CHF $482 438€ £366	706 CHF $758 689€ £576

<u>How to Obtain</u>: Order online. Several firms do sell these passes, but it is advised to purchase through the Swiss Pass site. When purchasing through www.Swiss-Pass.ch, it is much easier to resolve pass issues while in Switzerland than having to work through an online reseller. Purchase through www.Swiss-Pass.ch.

~ ~ ~ ~ ~ ~

6: Getting Around in Geneva

Walking, Trams, Buses, & Water Taxis

The right bank area and much of the city center of Geneva is level and relatively easy to walk around and find your way.

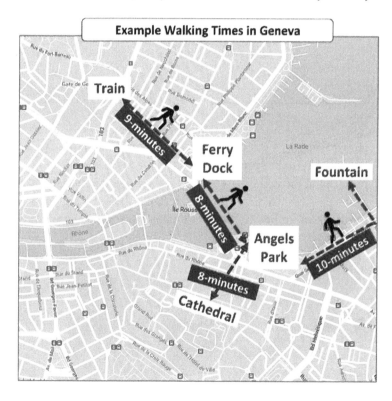

Trams in Geneva are in a variety of colors and makes.
Photo Source: Hoff1980-Wikimedia

Having two distinct "sides," the Right Bank and the Left Bank, makes it even easier to understand where places are located.

Geneva has a good mix of local transportation, and the systems are not complex to navigate or learn how to use. There are few "pedestrian only" areas, but this is still a safe city to explore on foot.

To reach the more popular attractions, which may be found throughout the city on both banks, a mix of walking and local transportation will likely be required. Some destinations, such as those around the United Nations, are a good distance from the center and trams are suggested.

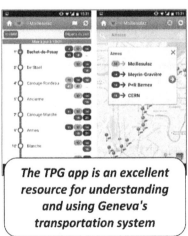

The TPG app is an excellent resource for understanding and using Geneva's transportation system

There is little need to have a car in town or even to travel to other towns or mountain adventures. The train and ferry systems are excellent, relaxing, and fun.

Any transportation system can be daunting at first and Geneva is no exception. **Actually, given the number of variables for tickets, it can be very confusing.**

The network of differing tram lines, buses, and ferries is quite comprehensive, but understanding it can take a little time. To help with this, **consider downloading the TPG app** to obtain full details on the routes, time schedules, and costs. You may even purchase and use tickets with this app.

Ticket Options and Prices:

Tickets cover travel on buses, trams, local ferries, and even local trains. Tickets have the variables of time, the zone traveled, class of ticket, and age bracket. The good news is that the ticket machines make it easy to determine which ticket to purchase.

> **Free Local Transportation**
>
> You do NOT need to purchase a transportation pass if you have a Geneva City Pass. Also, most area lodging provide free passes for the duration of your stay.

Tickets may be purchased from machines at all bus, tram, and ferry stops. Cash is suggested. One ticket covers all modes of transportation, so you do not have to purchase separate tickets for trams and buses. To simplify the purchase, consider buying a "Cart @bonus" pre-paid travel voucher from a local store. These vouchers available in different amounts and may be used to acquire a ticket at the machines. Doing this, removes the need to have correct change when buying tickets from a machine.

Time Options:

- Hour: Valid for 1 hour of travel starting from when you purchase the ticket. Caution, given that tickets are based on the time when they are purchased and not from when first used, do not buy tickets in advance for a return or future trip.

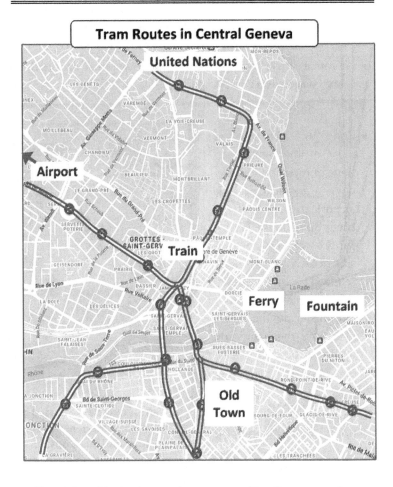

Tram Routes in Central Geneva

- <u>Short Hop:</u> Limited to a trip not exceeding 3 one-way bus or tram rides or one boat taxi ride. This ticket is not time-based, like the 1-hour ticket.

- <u>Day Pass:</u> Good for unlimited travel for 1 calendar day, not for a 24-hour period. Don't buy this pass if your travel starts later in the day as it is not timed from when your travel starts.

There are two versions: Full day starting from 5am or a shorter day where travel does not begin until 9am or later.

- If you are traveling on a weekend with a spouse or friend one Day Pass covers two people.

Zone Options:

- <u>Zone 10</u> – This covers most of the Swiss portions of metropolitan Geneva including the airport area. It does not cover travel to the French suburbs or very far outside of town. This is often referred to as a "Unireso" ticket as this is the agency administering these services and the name you will see on ticket machines.

- <u>Outside of Geneva:</u> Needed for most mountain adventures and for any travel into France. Variables include: (a) Léman Pass – allows for cross-border travel into France, or (b) for travel to other areas of Switzerland purchase either a ticket from SBB (the Swiss train system), or a Swiss Pass which covers most public transportation, including gondolas, throughout Switzerland.

> **Tickets may be purchased from these machines at all tram and bus stops. Instructions are simple to follow.**

Age Options:

There are two price tiers which vary by age: (a) Adult full-fare, and (b) Reduced rate for children and seniors. The rates for child and seniors are typically around half of a full adult fare.

Ticket Class Options:

Most travel has the options of 1st or 2nd class tickets. The One-Hour or Short Hop tickets are only available for 2nd class.

There are three price tiers which vary by age: Adult, Child, and Seniors. The rates for child and seniors are typically around 50% to 70% of a full adult fare

Example Ticket Prices for Geneva Zone Depicted in Swiss CHF rates as of March 2022.				
Ticket Type	Full Adult Fare		Child & Seniors	
	2nd Class	1st Class	2nd Class	1st Class
1 Hour	3 CHF	5.40 CHF	2 CHF	3.5 CHF
Short Hop	2 CHF	n/a	1.80 CHF	n/a
Day Pass	10 CHF	17 CHF	7.30 CHF	12.50CHF
Day Pass from 9am	8 CHF	13.60 CHF	5.60 CHF	9.60 CHF

Water Taxis:

One enjoyable and relaxing way to travel to and from Geneva's left and right bank is to take a water taxi.

These bright yellow boats, known as "Les Mouettes" (The Seagulls), travel all year. There are four lines simply numbered "M-1" through "M-4." Ticket prices are the same as local buses and trams and are

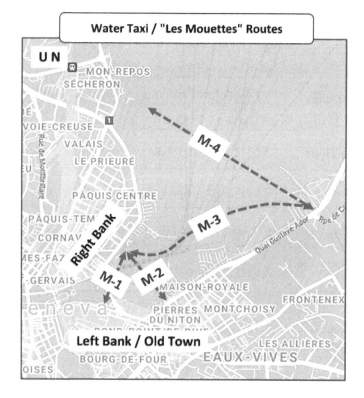

included in hourly or daily passes. As with other public modes of transportation, if you have a city pass or are staying in a local hotel, you can ride these relaxing taxis for no charge.

~ ~ ~ ~ ~

7: Shopping and Local Specialties

Geneva is a haven for upscale shopping in addition to the normal array of boutiques, gift shops, and department stores. The city is noted for quality watches, chocolate, and designer clothing boutiques.

While excellent shopping may be found throughout the city, for first-time visitors there are two similar shopping areas to pick from to find "all things Swiss."

Shopping and dining on the Left Bank
The Place de la Fusterie - Between Rue du Rhône and Rue du Marché.
Photo Source: Google Maps

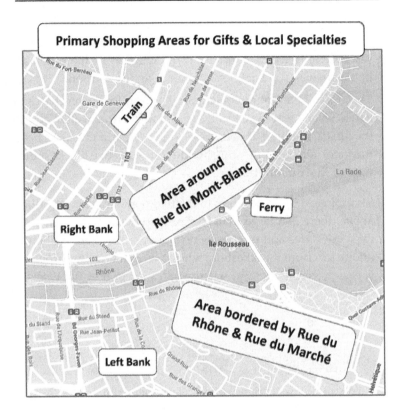

Primary Shopping Areas for Gifts & Local Specialties

Left Bank – City Center: This is the most notable area for shopping in Geneva. A great place to start is the section which rests along and close to the two main streets of Rue du Rhône and Rue du Marché. Everything you could want is here and there is no shortage of plazas with outdoor restaurants to add to the enjoyment. Once you are done shopping, head over to the Jardin Anglais Park along the lakeshore.

In addition to the numerous specialty stores such as Massimo Dutti or Benetton, the large Bongénie department store is a destination site for many. Place du Molard is a popular spot for shopping and numerous outdoor restaurants.

Right Bank – Rue du Mont-Blanc:[9] This broad avenue starts out from the Pont du Mont-Blanc (Bridge) on the right bank and bisects the area which houses several of Geneva's more notable hotels such as The Four Seasons and The Ritz-Carlton.

The stores here are a similar mix to those found on the right bank. Several leading chocolate shops are here as well to add to the fun of shopping. If you are seeking a department store, head to Manor, a large multi-store building situated two blocks southwest of Rue du Mont-Blanc.

Shopping Mall: In addition to the two popular areas described above, there is a large mall. **Balexert,** (www.Balexert.ch) with over 130 stores and numerous restaurants. This mall is about 4 kilometers from the lakeshore which places it near the airport. It is easy to reach via tram where you can get off at the Balexert stop.

Chocolate Shops

You are in Switzerland, and this is where you will find some of the best chocolates available anywhere. Numerous chocolate stores and kiosks are here and, without trying, you will come across them as you stroll the city.

---

[9] **Street Names Change Along a Route:** Very often in Geneva, you will find that major avenues change their name as you move along. In the case of Rue du Mont-Blanc, it is only a major avenue for 3 blocks and then the primary traffic flow takes a bend to become Rue de Chantepoulet which goes for a short distance and then changes names again. This same situation occurs with the Rue du Marché on the right bank.

Sample some of the world's finest chocolates at the
"Sweetzerland" shop on Rue du Mont-Blanc
Photo Source: Geneve.com

Some of these shops and chocolate factories stand above the rest and, if you love chocolate, one or more of the stores will likely be on your wish list to visit.

Right Bank Chocolate Shops:

- <u>Sweetzerland.</u> Located on rue du Mont-Blanc near the Pont du Mont-Blanc. The store makes many of their chocolates on site. www.Sweetzerland.net

- <u>La Chocolaterie de Genève</u>. On Rue des Alpes, a block south of the train station. www.La-Chocolaterie-de-Geneve.ch

- <u>Du Rhône Chocolatier Mont-Blanc</u>. On rue du Mont-Blanc, mid-way between the train station and the river. www.DuRhoneChocolatier.ch

- <u>Stettler & Castrischer</u>: They also have a shop in the city center, left bank area of town. The right bank shop is tucked back on the small street Rue de Berne. www.Stettler-Castrischer.com.

Left Bank Chocolate Shops:

- <u>Auer.</u> In the heart of the upscale shopping area and main shopping sector of town. Located on Rue de Rive. This is a great place to not only purchase chocolates, but to sit and have a cup of coffee to enjoy it. www.Chocolat-Auer.ch

- <u>Martel Chocolatier</u>. Also located in the heart of the upscale city center shopping area, near the popular Place du Molard. www.Martel-Chocolatier.ch.

- <u>Du Rhône Chocolatier</u>. They also have a shop on the right bank. This is a popular stop not just for chocolate, but light meals and coffee as well. www.DuRhoneChocolatier.ch

- <u>Teuscher</u>: Located a few blocks west of the main city center and the Pont du Mont-Blanc. This small chocolate shop is on Rue de la Corraterie and carries a selection of gifts in addition to chocolate. www.Teuscher-Zurich.ch.

Food Halls, Farmers Markets, & Local Craft Markets

Most cities in Europe have popular outdoor farmers or crafts markets and Geneva is no exception. These markets are a great way to sample local fare and do so without breaking the bank.

Five of the more popular markets in Geneva are listed here. Take note of the days and hours they are open as they are not all the same.

Right Bank – Place de la Navigation: A short walk from either the train station or the lakeshore, this small market offers an international array of food items. This neighborhood is called

Open Food and Craft Markets in Geneva

"Paquis" and is known as one of the more multi-cultural sections and the array of food offerings can reflect this. This market is open on Tuesday and Friday.

Left Bank - Plainpalais Market: One of the larger farmers markets in Geneva. Located on the large open plaza "Plaine de Palais" deep in the city's left bank shopping area. The best times to come here are on Sunday and Tuesday. This same open square also hosts a regular flea market on Saturdays and Wednesdays.

The Halle de Rive
A Large food hall in the Eaux-Vives section of the Left Bank
Photo Source: Geneve.com

Left Bank – Halle de Rive and Eaux-Vives Farmers Market:
Two open markets to explore here. One, the Halle de Rive, is an
enclosed mall with dozens of shops. The focus is local food specialties. It is a great place to pick up excellent prepared meals.

The other market held in this same "Eaux-Vives" area is on
Boulevard Helvétique. This outdoor market takes place on
Wednesdays and Saturday.

Left Bank – Place de la Fusterie: A smaller market in the heart
of the city center shopping area adjacent to Rue du Marché.
There is a mix of food stalls, crafts and souvenirs to be found
here.

Left Bank – Carouge Farmers Market: This market is a bit further out from the center of town, across the river Arve but is easily reached by tram. Coming here provides a great opportunity

to explore this quaint section of Geneva. This district was part of France up until 1816. The open market is large with a wide array of local delicacies. You will find many residents coming here to conduct their weekly shopping. This market is open on Wednesday and Saturday.

Fondue Restaurants

If you have the opportunity while in Geneva, consider having a fondue lunch or dinner. Many restaurants and cafes in Geneva offer this traditional Swiss delight. There are even dining options on boats to add to the fun.

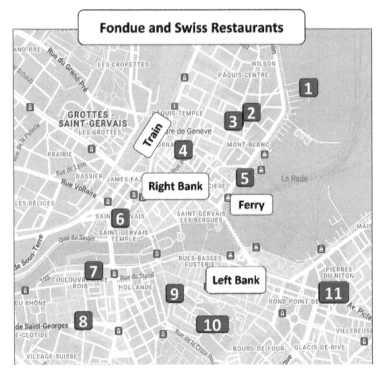

The great news with this meal is it does not have to be an outrageously expensive event. Some of the well-rated locations serving fondue are small and informal cafes and their costs are less expensive, although not cheap, than the more formal establishments.

Restaurants serving fondue can be found throughout the area. Listed here are several of the popular destinations which either specialize in fondue or their focus is Swiss cuisine and fondue is one of their top offerings.

Fondue Restaurants and Cafés	
Map #	Name, Address, Website, & Description
Right Bank	
1	Bateau Restaurant Privatisé Quai Wilson / www.HomeBoat.ch Casual dining on a boat. A bit pricey. Entire boat can be rented.
2	Restaurant Edelweiss Place de la Navigation 2 www.HotelEdelweissGeneva.com Fun, Swiss chalet style. Specializes in Fondue and classes are provided.
3	Auberge de Savièse Rue des Pâquis 20 / www.AubergeDeSaviese.com Swiss-chalet style restaurant in a warm, inviting atmosphere. Fondue and other Swiss specialties.
4	Au Petite Chalet Rue de Berne 17 / www.AuPetiteChalet.ch Casual bistro-style environment. Moderately priced with wide range of Swiss specialties.

Fondue Restaurants and Cafés	
Map #	**Name, Address, Website, & Description**
5	Les Fondues du Bateau Quai du Mont-Blanc 4 / LesFonduesDuBateau.com Fondue restaurant on a boat. A bit formal but only moderately priced.
6	Saint-Chervais Rue des Corps-Saints (No website found) Casual, café-style with outdoor seating available.
Left Bank	
7	Restaurant Coulouvrenière Rue de la Coulouvrenière 29/ (No website found) A bit rustic with a casual atmosphere and menu.
8	Le Gruyérien - Plainpalais Bd de Saint-Georges 65 / www.Bucherronne.ch Informal bistro serving a broad range of Swiss specialties.
9	Restaurant Le Boël-Chez Adriano Rue de la Tour-de-Boël 5 / (No website found) Casual atmosphere with outdoor seating available. Moderately priced.
10	Restaurant Les Armures Rue du Soleil-Levant / www.LesArmures.ch A bit upscale with nice outdoor seating available.
11	Café Bon-Vin Rue François-Versonnex 17 / www.CafeBonVin.ch Bistro style – informal. Moderate pricing.

8: Museums, Monuments, & Other Attractions

There is something here for every age and preference ranging from great museums to relaxing parks and historical structures.

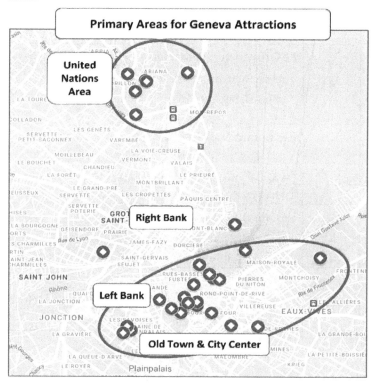

The good news is that a majority of the in-town attractions are clustered in the two areas of (a) near the United Nations and (b) in the Old Town and City Center area. The popular out-of-town mountain attractions are described in chapter 12.

United Nations Area

A cluster of popular attractions may be found near the United Nations complex. This area is easy to reach by tram and, once there, each attraction is only a short walk from the others.

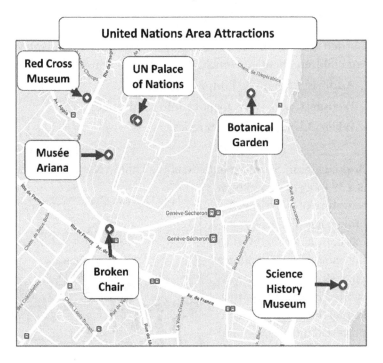

United Nations Area Attractions

Ariana Museum / Musée Ariana: A unique museum dedicated to the history of glass and ceramics. There are over 25,000 items devoted to pottery, stoneware, porcelain, China, and kiln craft.

Address: Avenue de la Paix 10, Geneva

Website: www.Ariana-Geneve.ch

When Open: Tuesday to Sunday from 10am to 6pm

Botanical Garden / Conservatoire et Jardin Botaniques: A great place to escape the busy city. With nearly 70 acres of grounds, there is a lot to see including over 16,000 different plant species in the outdoor gardens and expansive greenhouses. The Winter Garden and herbarium are some of the more popular displays. For children, there is an enchanted forest and carousel.

Address: Chemin de l'Impératrice 1

Website: Check www.Geneva.Info for details.

When Open: Tuesday to Sunday.

Broken Chair: Standing outside of the United Nations complex is a 39 foot (12 meter) high sculpture of a chair with a broken leg. There is no admission fee or facilities as this monument sits along a busy street. The chair was created by the Swiss artist, Daniel Berset in 1996 to protest land mines and cluster bombs.

Address: Ave de la Paix.

Broken Chair Monument
Photo Source: Google Maps

International Museum of the Red Cross and Red Crescent: Across the street from the UN Palace of Nations is the museum dedicated to the work and history of the Red Cross and its humanitarian efforts. Visitors may view a real-time display of active efforts throughout the world and see galleries highlighting the history of this important organization.

Address: Ave de la Pais 17, Geneva

Website: www.RedCrossMuseum.ch

When Open: Every day from 10am to 5pm except Monday.

Science History Museum / Musée d'Histoire des Sciences: Come here to gain an understanding of how our sciences have developed. This museum has an impressive collection of scientific instruments dating from the early 17th century. Exploring the exhibits provides helpful background on a broad range of sciences including astronomy, meteorology, microscopy, and more.

Address: Rue de Lausanne 128, Geneva

Website: www.Museum-Geneve.ch

When Open: Wednesday to Monday from 10am to 5pm.

United Nations & Palace of Nations: Tours of the Palais des Nations are available in addition to the ability to explore much of the grounds which are located on Ariana Park. For numerous reasons, this is a secure area and, to tour the facility, you must go on a guided group tour and pass through a rigid security check. Individuals are generally not able to go on the tour without joining a group.

This impressive and greatly important facility began construction in the 1920s and has continued to grow. Guided tours may be purchased from several providers such as Viator.com.

The UN Palace of Nations
Photo Source: Geneve.com

The picturesque array of flags from member nations may be visited from the street without having to enter through the security barriers.

Address for Tour Meeting Point: 14 Avenue de la Paix

Website: UNGeneva.org

Other Right Bank Attractions:

Not all sights on the right bank are in the United Nations area. There are several very different sites to consider visiting and three are closer to the heart of town. Four attractions are described here.

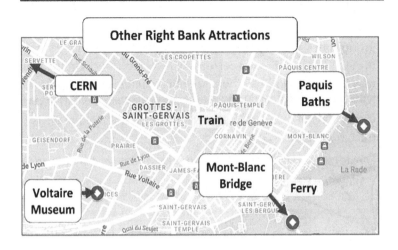

CERN Laboratories: The "European Organization for Nuclear Research" operates the world's largest particle physics laboratory. It is known for its "Large Hadron Collider" which is central to nuclear research.

This lab sits a short distance outside of central Geneva, in the town of Meyrin and a short distance from the Geneva airport. This massive facility sits on top of the border with France resulting in it being shared between the two countries. It may be reached from Geneva by tram.

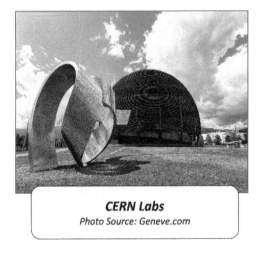

CERN Labs
Photo Source: Geneve.com

Guided tours of the labs are available both with structured group tours and individual tours. Individual's wishing to tour the facility must do so in person at CERN reception. Group tours may be booked online. Tours are not available every day so it is best to check the website to determine if they are available when you will be in town. Note that the tours do not include visits to the Large Hadron Collider.

Address: 1, Esplanade des Particules / Meyrin, Switzerland

Website: Visit.Cern

Mont-Blanc Bridge / Pont du Mont-Blanc: This large bridge over the Rhône is the main connector between the two sides of Geneva. It is generally very busy, but the pedestrian lanes on each side are safe and provide excellent photo opportunities of the city, the Jet d'Eau, and the ferries coming and going. All

Pont du Mont-Blanc spanning the Rhône River
Photo Source: Xavier-Wikimedia Commons

along the bridge are flags which always include Swiss and Geneva flags and sometimes include other flags to commemorate special events.

Adjacent to the bridge is a small island named the "Île Rousseau" named after famed 18th century philosopher and composer Jean-Jacques Rousseau. This little island-park is reached by floating bridges from either side of the river.

Pâquis Baths / Bains des Pâquis: A pool, bath, and sauna park located on a prominent jetty near the numerous large hotels which line Quai du Mont-Blanc. Portions of this facility are open all year which include a sandy beach, swimming pools, and spas. The services include swimming lessons, massages, and yoga classes. You may stroll out to the end of the jetty without having to enter the pool and spa facility. It is a popular spot for swimming in Lake Geneva from the jetty and beach.

Address: Quai du Mont-Blanc 30, Geneva

Website: Bains-Des-Paquis.ch

When Open: Hours vary by the season.

Voltaire Museum / Musée Voltaire de la Bibliothèque de Genève: This is combination library and museum dedicated to Voltaire a noted writer, scholar, and philosopher from the 18th century. There are over 20,000 works by and about Voltaire including writings and works of art. Group tours are available.

Address: Rue des Délices 25, Geneva

Website: Institutions.Ville-Geneve.ch

When Open: Monday through Saturday from 9am to 5pm

Left Bank (Old Town and City Center) Attractions:

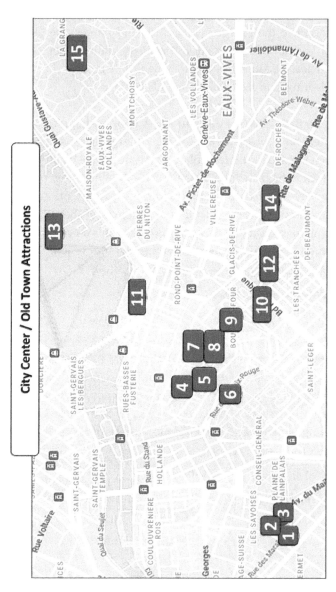

City Center / Old Town Attractions

Geneva's left bank which encompasses the Old Town and City Center sections is where a majority of the attractions, parks, and monuments are found. If you are staying in one of the many hotels on the right bank most of these can easily be reached by walking across the Mont-Blanc Bridge or taking local transportation across the river.

All attractions which follow have numbers which correspond to the map symbols on the previous page.

1 – MEG Ethonology Museum / Musée d'ethnographie de Genève: A museum dedicated to highlighting and exploring cultures around the world. There are numerous exhibits here focusing on various cultures. Throughout the year, the museum sponsors several concerts, shows, and workshops to help visitors understand the differences between cultures.

> Earned the **"European Museum of the Year"** award in 2017.

Address: Bd Carl-Vogt 65, Geneva

Website: www.Meg-Geneve.ch

When Open: Daily from 11am to 6pm – closed Monday.

2 – Modern Art Museum / MAMCO Genève: A 4-story building, which was once a laboratory, now houses an array of art from a variety of contemporary artists. The mix of exhibits can be confusing at first so consider joining one of the guided tours to help understand what you are viewing. Next door is the Centre for Contemporary Art.

Address: Rue des Vieux-Grenadiers 10, Geneva

Website: www.Mamco.ch

When Open: Daily from noon to 6pm – closed Monday

3 – Patek Philippe Museum: Touted as "A Temple to Watchmaking" this prestigious museum has over 2,500 items on display including some of the world's finest watches, miniatures, and watch making equipment. Visitors should take note there are restrictions on taking photos here. The collection is not limited to the Patek Philippe brand. The museum is easy to reach via tram and is close to the Modern Art Museum.

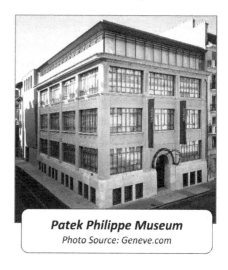

Patek Philippe Museum
Photo Source: Geneve.com

Address: Rue des Vieux-Grenadiers 7, Geneva

Website: www.PatekMuseum.com

When Open: Tuesday to Friday 2pm to 6pm. Saturday 10am to 6pm. Closed Sunday and Monday.

4 – Barbier-Mueller Museum / Musée Barbier-Mueller: This museum in the heart of Geneva's Old Town is focused on the arts from different cultures and civilizations of the world. It is tucked away on a quiet side street and easy to miss. The museum boasts the largest private collection of art from Asia, Africa, Oceania, and ancient civilizations.

Address: Rue Jean-Calvin 10, Geneva

Website: www.Barbier-Mueller.org

When Open: Daily from 11am to 5pm.

5 – Tavel House / Maison Tavel: The oldest house in Geneva. It was first built in the 12th century and completely rebuilt in the 14th century after a fire. Today it houses exhibits on Geneva's history with items relating to the city and area from the Middle Ages to the 19th century. One of the highlights is a large model of early 19th century Geneva, when the city still had a wall around it for protection.

Address: Rue due Puits-St-Pierre 6, Geneva

Website: Institutions.Ville-Geneve.ch

When Open: Daily from 11am to 6pm. Closed Monday.

6 – Reformers Wall / Mur des Réformateurs: A 100-meter long (About 330 feet) set of carvings; the "International Monument of

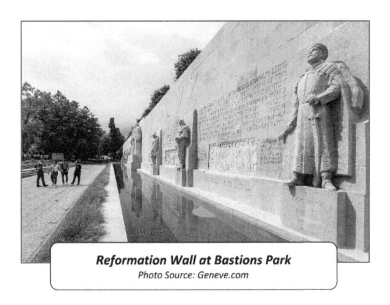

Reformation Wall at Bastions Park
Photo Source: Geneve.com

the Reformation" is dedicated to the Reformation. This was the period in the 16th century often cited as the Protestant Reformation when Martin Luther spawned the movement away from the Catholic Church. Calvinism began in Geneva among other similar reform movements. There are 10 statues here representing key "reformers." The wall is in Bastions Park which is a pleasant green space in the center of Geneva's Old Town. Built in 1917, this monument and park are very scenic and worth visiting. The International Museum of the Reformation is a short block northeast from here.

The "World's Longest Bench"
the "Promenade de la Treille"
parallels the Reformation wall.
Check it out just for fun.
Photo Source: Geneve.com

Address: Prom des Bastions 1, Geneva

7 – The International Museum of the Reformation / Musée International de la Réforme: Located in the same place where the Protestant Reformation was adopted in the early 16th century. It is this museum which provides background on this movement in history and the impact on life throughout Europe. The rooms in this museum and former mansion are arranged by themes and historical periods. A must for individuals interested in religious history.

Address: Rue du Cloître 4, Geneva

Website: www.Musee-Reforme.ch

When Open: TBD – as of this writing the museum is closed for extensive renovations.

8 – St. Peter Cathedral / Cathédrale Saint-Pierre-Geneve: This is one of the most visited monuments in Geneva and is referred to equally as Saint-Peter Cathedral or Saint-Pierre Cathedral. This cathedral which sits at a high spot in Geneva's Old Town was built in the 12th century. It is known as the home of the Protestant Calvinist movement. There are three elements to a visit: the cathedral itself; below the cathedral are crypts which is an active archeological site; and above the cathedral you may

You can view the city and lake from the top of the cathedral.

visit the towers. There is a fee to go up to the towers. Once there, the photo opportunities of the town below are tremendous.

If you wish to visit the towers, there are 157 steps to take and no elevator. The archaeological site includes items dating to prehistoric times.

Address: Cr de Saint-Pierre, Geneva

Website: www.Cathedrale-Geneve.ch

When Open: Visiting times vary by the season and day. In general, count on being able to tour from 10am to 5:30pm Monday to Saturday and in the afternoons on Sunday.

9 – **Place du Bourg-de-Four**: Close to the cathedral is Geneva's oldest square, the "Place du Bourg-de-Four," which dates to the 9th century. It has been an important marketplace for centuries and once stood just outside of the ancient city walls. Today, it remains the main square in Geneva's Old Town and is a great place to come to do some shopping and sit at one of the many cafés.

Address: Bourg-de-Four, Geneva

10 – **Museum of Art and History / Musée d'Art et d'Histoire**: Geneva's largest museum with over one million pieces. Consider renting an audio guide here as there is much to see. This large building has a very open feeling, and it does take a while to navigate through it. Allow several hours to see the major exhibit areas which focus on western history and art from prehistoric times to current day. Next to the museum is the "Promenade de l'Observatoire" which is a pleasant green space with good views of the town below.

Address: Rue Charles-Galland 2, Geneva

Website: www.Institutions.Ville-Geneve.ch

11 – English Garden / Jardin Anglais: This attractive park was started in the mid 1800's with the goal of improving how the harbor area looks. It was built in an English Garden style, the first in Geneva. This park is the first thing visitors come upon after crossing the main bridge, the Pont du Mont-Blanc. It has several noteworthy features including over 10,000 flowers, a monument to commemorate Geneva's incorporation into Switzerland, and the flower clock.

For photographers, this is a great spot to take photos of the Jet d'Eau and the right bank of the city. In the park, there is a restaurant, a café, and public restrooms.

Address: Quai du Général-Guisan 34, Geneva (Next to the Pont du Mont-Blanc)

Website: www.Geneve.ch/fr/Jardin-Anglais

When Open: Always open.

The Flower Clock at Jardin Anglais
Photo Source: Wikimedia

12 – Russian Orthodox Church / Église Russe: The golden domes of this ornate building in the upper area of Geneva's Old Town beckon visitors. This small church was built in 1859 and is considered to be one of the city's more appealing buildings. It is open for visitors but note that photography is prohibited.

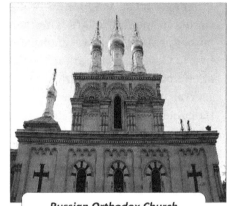

Russian Orthodox Church
Photo Source: Björn S-Wikimedia Commons

Address: Rue Rodolphe-Toepffer 9, Geneva

Website: www.EgliseRusse.ch

When Open: The best times to visit are from 11am to 5pm except Monday.

13 – Geneva Water Jet / Jet d'Eau: The city's most noted landmark by any measure. This impressive water jet (or fountain – both terms are used frequently) pushes a jet of water up to 460 feet (140 meters). Over 130 gallons of water are pumped upward every second at a speed of 125 miles per hour (200 km). The fountain operates during the day all year but there are times in severe weather when it is temporarily halted.

The current version of the fountain was put in place in 1951. Previous versions were less powerful, and the first version was closer into town. The fountain is generally limited to daylight hours although during special celebrations it does operate and is fully illuminated.

You can get close to the base of the Water Jet

Photo Source: Björn S-Wikimedia Commons

Visiting the fountain is fun, although you should expect to get wet if you get close. Surprisingly, visitors may get very close to the base of the fountain. It is out on a long jetty (the Je-tée-des Eaux-Vives) and there is no admission fee. Near the entrance to the jetty is an outdoor café which provides a good place to sit and watch the fountain and neighboring marina.

Address: Quai Gustave-Ador, Geneva

14 – Natural History Museum / Musée d'Histoire Naturelle: Switzerland's largest natural history museum. The focus is on the world of plants and animals with many exhibits on the region's flora and fauna. Hundreds of stuffed animals are on display. The earthquake simulator, which takes you into a shaking kitchen, is an interesting experience.

Address: Rte de Malagnou 1, Geneva

Website: Institutions.Ville-Geneve.ch

When Open: Open every day except Monday from 10am to 5pm

15 – La Grange Park / Parc de La Grange: A short walk east from the water jet and the city center is an open park which is a pleasure to explore on a summer day. The grounds include a rose garden, ponds, a forested area, and several meandering walkways. There are also public restrooms. In the center, on a rise with good views of the lake, is a manor house which had been built in the late 18trh century. During the summer, several outdoor concerts are held on the grounds.

Address: Quai Gustave-Ador, Geneva

Website: www.Ville-Geneve.ch

When Open: 6am to 10pm

La Grange Park viewed from the manor house.
Photo Source: Wikimedia Commons

~ ~ ~ ~ ~ ~

9: Lake Geneva Ferries and Towns

When visiting Geneva, it is hard to miss the beautiful sight of the historic (early 20th century) ferries coming and going from the docks near the city. In addition to the bright yellow Mouette water taxis, there is a fleet of larger white and red ferries which take passengers to many towns along the lake.

Lake Geneva (Lac Léman) is one of the largest lakes in Europe and, with many snow-capped mountains bordering it, is a

One of the classic ferries on Lake Geneva
Photo Source: Geneve.com

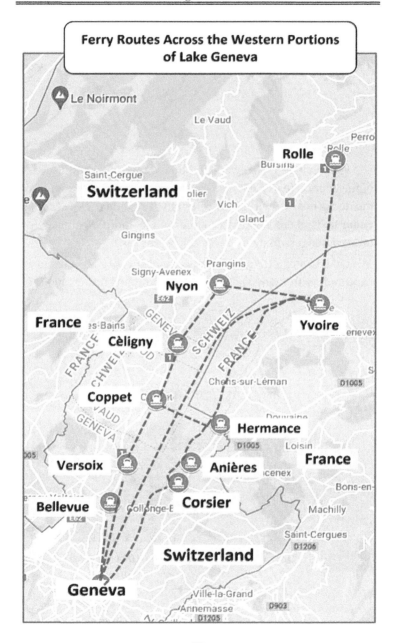

Ferry Routes Across the Western Portions of Lake Geneva

Take the ferry to Lausanne from Geneva?

Generally, this is not advised as it is a 3 hour and 45-minute ferry ride – vs taking a 45-minute train trip.

delight to experience by boat. There are two main options for traveling on these boats: (a) as transportation to another town on the lake; or (b) for a casual tour or dinner cruise out of central Geneva.

The fleet of ferries operate all year (weather permitting) with a greater number of departures during the summer months. The ferries serve numerous towns along the lake including several French towns.

Bicycles may be brought on board any of these ferries to add to the fun. None of the ferries carry automobiles. All ferries are handicapped accessible.

To visit one of the towns by ferry for a day excursion (a recommended experience), it is helpful to note the following:

- The number of departures daily is limited so you may want to plan a trip in which you take the ferry in one direction to your destination and then a bus or train for the other direction. Some lines such as the one between Nyon and Yvoire run frequently. Most routes travel only 1 or 2 times per day.

- You do not need to travel the full distance to Lausanne or Montreux. It can be fun to get off at one of the small towns along the way. (See the table starting on the next page.)

- The towns where ferries stop between Geneva and Lausanne (or Montreux) will differ by which departure you select.

- Ferries do have restrooms and snack bars on board.

- Most ferries depart from the dock on Geneva's right bank, the "Geneva Mont-Blanc" terminal. Some departures leave from one of two docks on the left bank, either the Eaux-Vives or Jardin-Anglais terminals. The departure point is clearly marked when you select your ticket.

> **Ticket Purchase Site**
>
> Recommend using the **GCN.ch** site to view departure schedules and buy tickets.

- Tickets are available in first and second class. First class tickets allow access to the upper deck which is partially open and provides great photo opportunities. First Class tickets typically cost around 50% more than 2nd class tickets.

- During the summer months, purchase tickets well in advance if possible, as this is a popular activity and can fill up early.

Following is a list of towns visited by the ferries on the western half of Lake Geneva. This list is limited to the western portion simply because the travel time by ferry to the eastern half can be more than most individuals would want for a day trip. If you will be staying the night in Lausanne or Montreux, then a one-way ferry trip could be considered.

Ferry Stops on western Lake Geneva			
Town Name	Ferry Travel Time from Geneva [10]	Town Population	Train or Bus Available To/From Town
Anières, CH	35 min	2,500	Bus

---

[10] **Ferry Travel Time**: Data source used is rome2Rio.com as of April 2022.

Ferry Stops on western Lake Geneva			
Town Name	Ferry Travel Time from Geneva [10]	Town Population	Train or Bus Available To/From Town
Bellevue, CH	25 min	3,300	Bus & Train
Cèligny, CH	1 hr	800	Train
Coppet, CH	45 min	3,100	Train
Corsier, CH	30 min	2,100	Bus
Hermance, CH	45 min	1,100	Bus
Nyon, CH	1 hr 15 min	21,000	Bus & Train
Rolle, CH	2 hr	6,300	Bus & Train
Versoix, CH	30 min	13,400	Bus & Train
Yvoire, FR	1 hr 30 min	1,100	Bus

Not every town on the above table and shown on the previous map will have the elements many individuals will want for a day trip such as historical sights, interesting streets to stroll, and cafes. Many ferry stops are simply nice small towns to live in, but not necessarily appealing to tourists nor do they cater to tourism.

Some of the more noted lakeside towns are best reached by train or car as the travel time by ferry can be lengthy. Information on these suggested day trips follows further in this chapter.

Two towns on western Lake Geneva are outlined here and are close enough for good day trips by ferry. In each case, they will offer visitors a variety of experiences and they are easy to reach by train or bus for the return portion of the trip.

Yvoire, France: This small town is one of the more popular destinations on western Lake Geneva. Established in the 14th century, Yvoire maintains a medieval feel even today. When you travel here by ferry, it is a short walk past an attractive marina to a pleasant maze of narrow streets lined with shops and restaurants. There is a delightful ancient feel about this town.

The Medieval Town of Yvoire, France

The Yvoire Chateau Castle Yvoire) provides for some photo opportunities. It is still owned by the Yvoire family and not open for tours.

Another highlight of the town is the ornate "Labyrinth-Garden of the Five Senses."

If you choose to travel from (or to) Yvoire by bus, the stop is on the highway which is roughly an 8-minute walk from the heart of Yvoire. Bus schedules vary by the day and season so check a site such as rome2Rio.com for the schedule matching when you will be there. Another travel option is to take the short ferry ride from Yvoire to Nyon and take the train into Geneva for the final leg of your travel. The Yvoire-Nyon ferry route runs frequently so waits for the next crossing are generally short.

> **Nyon and Yvoire Combined Trip**
>
> Consider visiting both Nyon and Yvoire on the same day trip. It is easy and fun to do.

Website: www.Visit-Yvoire.com

Nyon Switzerland: Nyon is located midway between Geneva and Lausanne. It is easily beached by ferry or train. There is also a frequent, smaller ferry which regularly crosses Lake Geneva to Yvoire. When arriving by ferry, you dock right in the heart of the lakefront district and there is a tourist office kiosk at the dock to provide local information. The lakeshore promenade is lined with shops, restaurants, and hotels. It is a laid-back, charming town which invites you to take long strolls.

Among the highlights of the town are the Castle of Nyon (Chateau de Nyon) and Roman ruins which include a small museum. The castle, built in the 12th century, is open for tours. The castle

Nyon, Switzerland
Photo Source: Google Earth

and museum are both a short walk from the ferry although it is an uphill walk.

If you choose to come or go by train, the station "Gare de Nyon" is a 10-minute walk from the lakeshore and ferry terminal. Caution, it is uphill much of the way from the lake.

Tourist Office Website: Nyon-Tourisme.ch

~ ~ ~ ~ ~ ~

Visiting Towns along the Eastern Portion of Lake Geneva:

Several of the more popular destinations on Lake Geneva will be found along the eastern shores of the lake. These towns and one castle are all accessible by ferry, but this is generally not advised for a day trip because of the travel time involved.

The following table highlights five daytrip destinations to consider from Geneva. Each of these are accessible by train, car, or ferry and each of these destinations offer the visitor noteworthy scenery and experiences. In each case, roundtrips from Geneva by train are easy to do in a day as multiple daily departures will be available.

> **Train Schedules**
>
> Check rome3Rio.com or other travel sites for current schedules and ticket purchase options.

Towns to Explore along eastern Lake Geneva		
Town Name	**Population**	**Train Travel Time from Geneva**
Chillon Castle, CH	n/a	1 hr 20 min
Évian-les-Bains, FR	9,100	50 min
Lausanne, CH	139,000	45 min
Montreux, CH	26,000	1 hr 10 min
Vevey, CH	17,000	1 hr 10 min

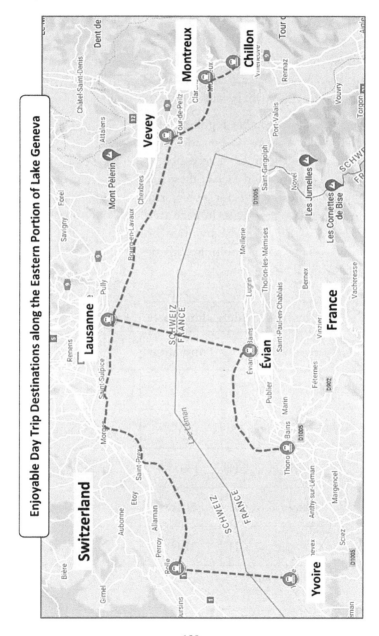

Enjoyable Day Trip Destinations along the Eastern Portion of Lake Geneva

Chillon Castle, Switzerland / Château du Chillon: This chateau is one of Lake Geneva's most iconic sights. It is near the farthest point on the lake from Geneva, but still reachable by train or car in under 90 minutes. It is officially located in the town of Veytaux and within walking distance to Montreux. The train stop for coming to the castle is between the castle and Veytaux. It is a five-minute walk from either the ferry or train terminals.

Chillon Castle
Easily Reached by Ferry or Train

The castle sits on a rocky promontory giving it a broad view of the lake and neighboring mountains. The building was crafted and updated over several centuries. It was started in the 12th century with add-ons and modifications ever since.

To enter, a ticket must be purchased and during high season this should be done in advance. You may choose from a self-guided tour or guided group tour. Allow two hours or more to visit the chateau and consider taking time to enjoy a break in the café.

Castle website: www.Chillon.ch

Évian-les-Bains, France: Often termed a "high market" resort town, Evian-les-Bains (Evian Baths) is an impressive town to visit. There is no doubt when strolling the pristine streets that this town caters to a wealthy clientele. The Evian name is also known around the world for its upscale mineral water.

This is not an ancient town as most of the prominent buildings such as the thermal baths, casino, town hall, and museum were built in the late 19th through early 20th century.

Come here to stroll along the casino area which faces the lake then head to the Plaza Charles de Gaulle where there are numerous small shops and frequent open markets.

Evian-les-Bains, France
Photo Source: Daniel Jolivet-Wikimedia Commons

When traveling to here, the ferry terminal is a short 5-minute walk to the casino and neighboring Palais Lumière, an impressive art and history museum. The train station (Gare d'Évian-les-Bains) is a bit further out and is roughly a 15-minute walk into town. If you take the train from Geneva, it is likely that it will depart Geneva from the Eaux-Vives station on the left bank and not the primary station across the lake.

One enjoyable travel option is to take the ferry from Evain-les-Bains to Lausanne. It is a short 30-minute ferry ride with frequent departures. From there, you can easily reach the Lausanne train station for the return leg of your trip.

Evian-les-Bains Website: **www.Evian-Tourisme.com**

~ ~ ~ ~ ~ ~

Lausanne, Switzerland: There is a lot to see and do in this small city. With this in mind, the next chapter covers the highlights of Lausanne instead of a brief synopsis here.

~ ~ ~ ~ ~ ~

Montreux, Switzerland & the Swiss Riviera: This area often referred to as "The Swiss Riviera" or "The Montreux Riveria" has been a haven for famous individuals such as Charlie Chaplin of silent film fame or Freddie Mercury from the rock group Queen who have lived here. Even Igor Stravinski composed his famous ballet "The Rite of Spring" here. The area is stunning and has a pleasant microclimate. It includes not only the charming small city of Montreux, but Chillon Castle and the town of Vevey as well.

Like Évian-les-Bains across the lake on the French side, this area caters to the well-heeled which fits right in with the moniker of "Swiss Riviera." Still, even for the budget-minded, this is an enjoyable region to visit and, if your schedule allows, consider staying a night or two here.

The Montreux lakeside promenade is lined with upscale hotels.
Photo Source: Wikimedia Commons

Montreux is at the heart of this area. It is easy to combine a visit here with a visit to Vevey or Chillon Castle as they are near each other. There is even a promenade along the lakeshore which enables visitors to walk all the way from Vevey, through Montreux and finish at Chillon Castle.

There is something for everyone in Montreux ranging from world-renowned festivals to mountain explorations, explorations of area vineyards, or chocolate tours.

The long lakeside promenade is one of the town's most popular attractions and, given the great views, it is easy to see why. One of the popular stops along here is the Freddie Mercury statue. Consider visiting the Queen studio which is upstairs in the casino. Another fun attraction is the chocolate train which takes visitors to the nearby Nestle factory.

If you travel to Montreux by train or ferry, both terminals are right in the center of town, so your explorations can begin immediately. Consider, for some added fun, taking the train into Montreux and then catch a ferry back to Lausanne for a full experience. A ferry ride along this section of the lake provides great photo opportunities.

Full details on Montreux and the area may be found at: www.MontreuxRiviera.com.

Vevey, Switzerland: This part of the Swiss Riveria is popular for many reasons. In addition to the views of mountains across the lake, you can explore wineries and even take a funicular up to the local peak.

Vevey, Switzerland Funicular

A surprise to many is to learn that Nestle is headquartered here and their large office complex can't be missed. Leading attractions include the lakeside promenade which extends to and beyond Montreux, a statue to Charlie Chaplin, and specialty museums such as the Swiss Camera Museum.

The Vevey funicular takes visitors on an 11-minute ride up to Mount-Pèlerin. Once at the top, you are roughly 2,300 feet (700 meters) above the lake. At the top, there is a small hotel, restaurant, and overlook. The funicular station is on the northwestern edge of town and about a 15-minute walk, but local buses are available and frequent.

Full details may be found on the joint Montreux and Vevey tourist office website at: www.MontreuxRiviera.com.

~ ~ ~ ~ ~ ~

10: Visiting & Exploring Lausanne

Lausanne[11], a small but bustling city of roughly 140,000, can be either an excellent and simple day trip from Geneva, or a good destination to stay overnight.

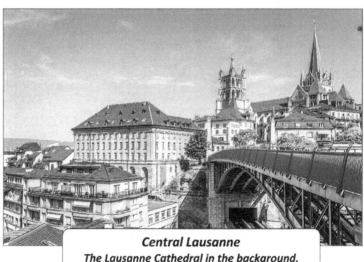

Central Lausanne
The Lausanne Cathedral in the background.

---

[11] **Lausanne Pronunciation:** The most common pronunciation is "Low-Zahn." Some sources provide slight variations to this.

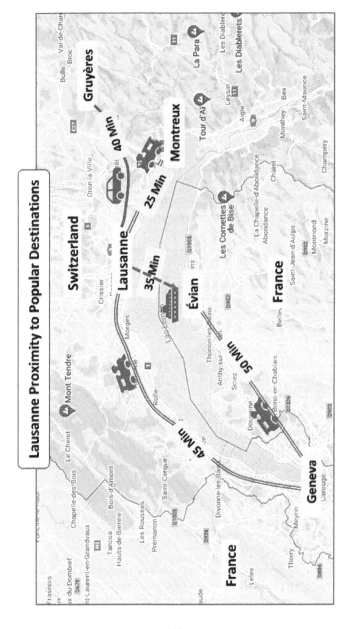

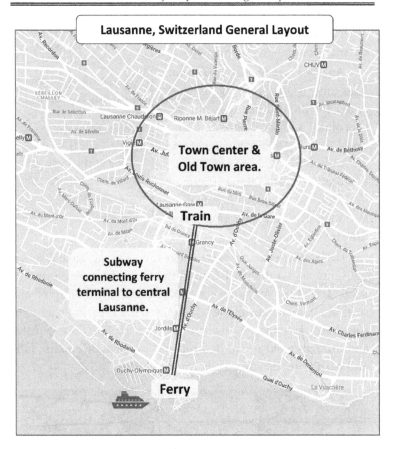

It is the fifth largest city in Switzerland and the capital of the canton Vaud. One of the notable aspects of Lausanne is that it is considered to be the "Olympic Capital." This is where the International Olympic Committee is based. There is even an Olympic Museum here.

If you choose an overnight stay in Lausanne, this is a good basecamp for explorations all along the Swiss Riveria (the area ranging from Vevey to the Chillon Castle). These explorations can be done by train or ferry. See the maps on the preceding pages.

Another enjoyable trip from Lausanne is to Gruyères, a town noted for its Middle Ages appeal, chocolates and local cheese. Many tours to Gruyères from Lausanne are available or you can rent a car to explore the area. Taking a tour to Gruyères from Geneva is generally not advised due to the long travel time involved.

Get a City Map

Lausanne is a complex city to explore. Consider picking up a map from the tourist office. There is an office at the train station and one near the ferry terminal.

Unlike Geneva and many other towns along Lake Geneva, Lausanne is not oriented around the lake and does border the lake. Most of the shopping and attractions are further uphill and several kilometers from the lakeshore. It is a hilly town and this soon becomes apparent to visitors as they explore the expansive and attractive old town. Be prepared to encounter many hilly and narrow roads while exploring the historic area.

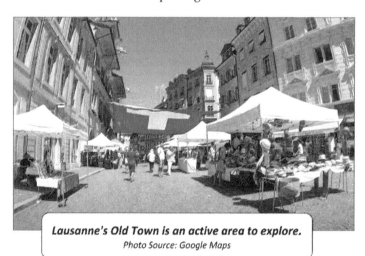

Lausanne's Old Town is an active area to explore.
Photo Source: Google Maps

Lausanne Tourism Website

Lausanne has a helpful website which provides a detailed map of the city plus information on hotels, dining, transportation, and more.

www.Lausanne-Tourisme.ch

Traveling to Lausanne:

The quickest travel option from Geneva is by train. Trains travel the route to Lausanne frequently which greatly increases flexibility in trip scheduling. When arriving in Lausanne, the station is uphill by nearly 2 kilometers from the lake and near the heart of town. The city's subway stops here which can be beneficial. Walking into the heart of town is between 5 to 10 minutes, depending on your destination.

If you choose to travel by ferry from Geneva, this is delightful, but slow. Consider making only one leg of a roundtrip journey by ferry and taking a train the other way. The ferry terminal is below the town and a greater distance than most individuals would want to walk to reach the city center. The subway/tram lines stop immediately next to the ferry terminal making travel into town very easy. Recommendation: Take the subway to the **"Riponne M Béjart"** station. This subway station is adjacent to the palace and it makes for a great location to start explorations.

Take the ferry to Lausanne from Geneva?

Generally, this is not advised for roundtrips as it is a 3 hour and 45-minute ferry ride vs taking a 45-minute train trip.

Lausanne Attractions:

Most of Lausanne's leading attractions are in the central city (Old Town) and easy to reach on foot. The most notable "attraction" is the historic area itself with its many narrow and hilly streets lined with shops and restaurants. Listed here are 5 sights which provide a variety of experiences and can easily be incorporated into a daytrip from Geneva.

Cathedral of Notre-Dame: A 13th century cathedral which was a noted stop along "The Way of Saint-James." This is the now very popular trail which ends in northwestern Spain. Highlights of this imposing church include a massive 6,000 pipe organ, the crypt, and 105 stained-glass panels. For individuals with strong legs, a hike to the tower (La Tour de Beffroi) provides nearly 360 views of the city, lake, and nearby mountains. For an interesting experience, each evening a night watchman calls out the time from the tower. This is a tradition that has lasted for 600 years.

Address: Place de la Cathédrale, Lausanne

Website: www.Cathedrale-Lausanne.ch.

Olympic Museum: With the Olympics organization based here, it is only natural that a museum dedicated to the history of the Olympics is in Lausanne. It is an expansive museum with displays on the history of the games, Olympic torches, clothing from previous events, and film clips. This museum is not close to the center of town, rather

Torches on display in the Olympic Museum
Photo Source: I.Inisheer - Wikimedia Commons

it is closer to the lakeshore and the ferry terminal.

Address: Quai d'Ouchy 1, Lausanne

Website: Olympic.org.

Sauvabelin Tower: On the northern edge of Lausanne is a large park, the Sauvabelin Park (or Bois de Sauvabelin). It is on a hill overlooking the area. A highlight for many is the 35meter tall (114 feet) wooden tower. It is generally open during daylight hours. The distance of nearly 3km uphill from the town center is more than most individuals want to do, but the city bus may be taken to within a few feet of the tower.

Sauvabelin Tower
Photo Source:
Tschubby - Wikimedia Commons

Address: 1018 Lausanne

Website: Tour-de-Sauvabelin-Lausanne.ch

Platform 10 Art Museums: Next to Lausanne's train station is a new group of three art museums with the interesting name of "Platform 10." The area where this new facility is located is also considered to be the main arts district for the city. Platform 10's collection of museums include:

- The Lausanne Cantonal Museum of Fine Arts – housing thousands of works of art.
- The Photo Elysée museum of photography
- Museum of Design and Contemporary Art

Address: Place de la Gare 16, Lausanne

Website: Platforme10.ch.

Old Bishop's Palace & Lausanne Historical Museum: Adjacent to the cathedral, in a palace built in the 11th century, is a modest museum which presents the history of the city and area. Among the attractions are large models of the city and surrounding countryside.

Address: Place de la Cathédrale 4, Lausanne

Website: Lausanne.ch

~ ~ ~ ~ ~ ~

11: Annecy Day Trip

A short distance south of Geneva is the city of Annecy. This community of over 130,000 is a noted destination and visitors from Geneva and cities along the Mediterranean often flock here to visit the riverfront, quaint streets, and beautiful lake. The Old Town and the lakeshore, a short walk from there, are excellent areas for photographers to get some notable photos.

Given the proximity to Geneva, it is easy to take either a half-day or full-day trip to Annecy. Several agencies such as

Enjoy one of many restaurants along Le Thiou River in central Annecy.
Photo Source: Dmitry A Motti - Wikimedia Commons

Viator.com and VisitACity.com offer these tours ranging from group bus tours to private excursions.

One caution for visitors who are crowd averse. Annecy is popular and in the high season can be very crowded.

Annecy sits at the northern end of Lake Annecy (Lac d'Annecy), the third largest lake in France, which stretches south for nine miles. This lake is one of the clearest in Europe. If you have time, go out on the lake using one of the many options available including: rental paddle boats; water taxis; and ferries to other lakeside towns

Traveling to Annecy:

In addition to the many structured tours, this is an easy city to reach from Geneva by car, bus, or train.

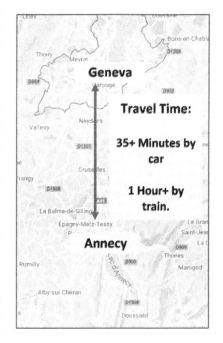

Travel by Car: If you have a rental car, the drive takes travelers along a pleasant country stretch, much of which is on the A41 highway. Driving time will typi-cally be between 35 to 45 minutes.

Once in Annecy, head to the parking garage at the Hôtel de Ville. This large structure and plaza are near the lakeside parks. From there, the lakeshore, Old Town, ferry port, and city center are all very close.

<u>Important:</u> Annecy is in France, so bring Euros with you. Also have your passport handy, just in case.

Travel by Train: Trains run frequently between Annecy and Geneva. It is important to note that if you have a Geneva Pass, it does not provide free travel on this route into France. Separate tickets will be required. Check www.SNCF.com or www.rome2Rio.com for schedules and online ticket purchases.

Most trains from Geneva to Annecy depart from the Eaux-Vives station near Geneva's city center on the left bank. When you arrive in Annecy, the station is roughly a ten-minute walk to the heart of the Old Town and an additional five-minute walk to the lakeshore. The walk takes you through the heart of Annecy's shopping district and is a pleasant and level trek.

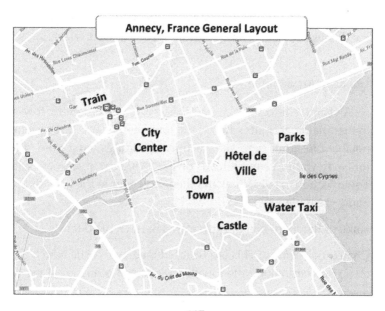

Annecy, France General Layout

A highlight of Annecy is the lakeshore where you can rent a small boat or take a boat tour.
Photo Source: Alex Brown - Wikimedia Commons

For detailed information on Annecy and the lake area, check out the region's website at: www.Lac-Annecy.com. For individuals wishing to get out into nature or explore the lake area in depth, the details provided on this site are a good place to start.

Annecy Attractions:

A visit to Annecy is like other historical, visitor-centric towns in that the biggest attraction is the town itself. There are several notable museums here and historical buildings. First-time visitors may want to simply focus on exploring the area in the Old Town section (Vielle Ville) and then head over to the lake for the many great views.

Some of the more notable attractions in town include:

Château d'Annecy: This is a restored medieval castle which sits on a rise overlooking the town and lake and offers good views of the nearby Alps. Inside the museum-castle complex are a mix of exhibits on local history, arts, and local natural history. Allow for an hour to see the museum's highlights. One caution, the 5-minute walk from old town is largely uphill.

Address: 5 Place du Château, Annecy

Website: www.Musees.Annecy.fr

The Island Palace in Annecy's old town.
Photo Source: Paul Hermans - Wikimedia Commons

Palais de l'Île / Island Palace: This small medieval palace was built on a rocky outcropping on the river Le Thiou in the heart of old Annecy. It is an iconic and frequently photographed sight. Over time, it has served as a fort, a prison, and a courthouse. Today, it is history museum and exposition center and is open to visitors to explore.

Address: 3 Pass de l'Île, Annecy

Website: www.Musees.Annecy.fr

Jardins de l'Europe: On the edge of town, partially surrounded by the lake and near the Hôtel de Ville, is a large and open park. During the summer months, you may find fairs and art shows in progress. It is intended to be a place of relaxation. Several sculptures adorn the gardens.

Address: Quai Napoléon III, Annecy

Website: www.Lac-Annecy.com

Pont des Amours / The Bridge of Loves: At the entrance to the Canal du Vassé from the lake, is a beautiful iron bridge built in 1859 which connects the Jardins de l'Europe with a large open city park Le Pâquier d'Annecy. This is a popular spot for photography of the bridge and from the bridge. Many weddings are held here. Near here are several boat-rental services.

Address: Canal du Vassé 74000, Annecy:

Boat Rental: This is a beautiful lake in a delightful mountain-backed setting, so why not get out on a boat to enjoy it. Along the large city park just north of city center (Le Pâquier d'Annecy), are several firms which rent everything from peddle boats to power craft. You can rent for as little as 30-minutes up to a half day. One of the bigger firms is Nautic Annecy www.Nautic-Annecy.com.

~ ~ ~ ~ ~ ~

12: Mont Blanc & Salève Adventures from Geneva

The sight of mountains and tall hills around Geneva beckon travelers to come visit and explore them. While many of the region's most noted mountains are a bit beyond a simple day trip, there are several near the city ranging from Salève which provides an enjoyable overlook

If you will be doing more than just short, casual hiking, consider downloading one of the many great trail and hiking guide apps such as Switzerland Mobility.

Mont Blanc & Le Môle - seen from Geneva
Photo Source: Geneve.com

of Geneva to Mont-Blanc, the highest mountain in the Alps.

Of the numerous mountains and ski areas around Geneva, two are outlined here as they are easy to reach for a relaxing day trip from Geneva and individuals with limited ability can enjoy them.

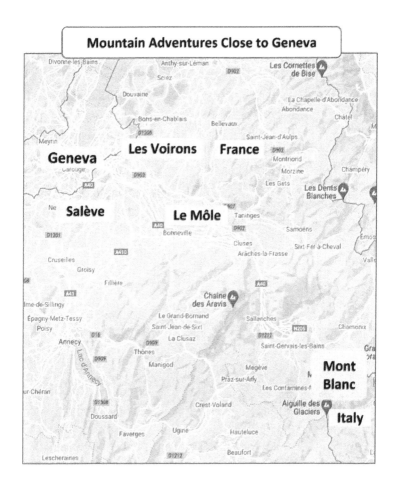

Mountain Adventures Close to Geneva

Important – both Mont-Blanc and Mont Salève are in France so you will need Euros, not Swiss Francs. Also, bring your passport in the off chance that it is checked at the France-Switzerland border.

Other nearby mountain areas such as Le Môle or Les Voirons (See map on the previous page) are more geared to hiking or skiing and not simple, relaxing day trips. Facilities at these two mountains are limited, so you may want to pack a lunch. Several websites provide great details on nearby mountains, how to access them, and various hiking routes. One excellent site for this is on the TouringSwitzerland.com site, then go to the sections on closest mountains near Geneva.

Suggested Mountain Adventures Near Geneva			
Mountain	Elevation	Travel Time to base from Geneva	Public Transport Available to Mountain?
Mont Salève, FR	1,097 M 3,600 Ft	20-30 min	Yes - Bus
Mont Blanc, FR	4,807 M 15,774 Ft	1 hr+ (Chamonix)	Shuttle Bus is best

Mont Salève:

Although not exceptionally high, this long mountain ridge provides excellent views of Geneva in one direction and Mont-Blanc in the other. At the top of the cable car line, is an overlook with an observation deck and outdoor restaurant. Several easy trails start out from here. If you wish, there is a trail leading back

View of Geneva from Mont Salève
Photo Source: Geneve.com

down the hill. A short walk from the upper station for the cable car is a French Restaurant with a tall observation tower.

<u>Traveling by Cable Car</u>: One caution: As of this writing, the cable car to Mont Salève is being rebuilt and is not scheduled to open until mid-2023. Visitors are advised to check the website at www.TelepheriqueduSaleve.com to determine availability.

When the cable car is running, this is the easiest and most enjoyable way to reach Salève's crest. Getting to the base of the cable car in the town of Étrembières, France is fairly simple, although the instructions may seem difficult at first.

1. Take the bus from Geneva to the Veyrier-Douane stop in Switzerland. This will be a 20 to 25-minute trip, depending on your starting point.
2. Walk across the border into France to the cable car station. It has the long name of "Téléphérique du Salève." This is less than a 10-minute walk along a pleasant and well-marked route.

3. If you have a rental car, there is a large parking lot at the cable car station.

Traveling by car from Geneva: It is roughly a 30-minute drive from central Geneva to the upper cable car station. The address is "Rte des 3 Lacs, Monnetier-Mornex, France." A caution, portions of the drive are along a narrow, steep, and winding mountain road so take care in the winter.

Mont-Blanc and Chamonix:

The town of Chamonix, combined with all that the Mont-Blanc range has to offer, is a heaven for any person wanting to experience the beauty and activities provided by nature. The adventure here begins with a visit to Chamonix, France. This is a resort

Chamonix with Mont-Blanc looming over it.
Photo Source: Arnaud 25 - Wikimedia Commons

town of 8,600 which sits at an elevation of 3,300 feet (1,000 meters) in a valley with steep mountains on either side.

Mont-Blanc towers over Chamonix with its elevation of 15,774 feet (4,807 meters). The destination point is an observation station called "Aiguille du Midi" which sits at 12,600 feet (3,840 meters). This station offers visitors an exciting array of places to explore ranging from viewing platforms, tunnels, a glass skywalk, and a walkway which circles the summit. There is also a restaurant and giftshop in this building complex.

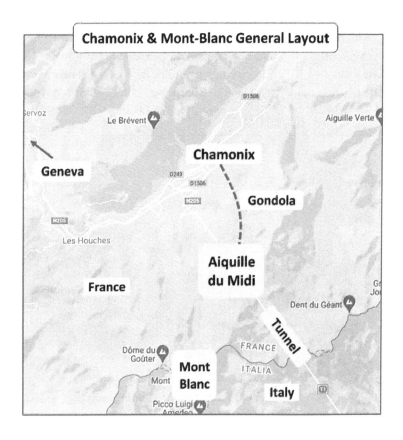

The Gondola: Due to safety con-straints, the main set of gondolas out of Chamonix to Aiquille du Midi does not run all year. It is open during summer but is likely to be closed in the winter and shoulder months. The operating schedule is posted on the **www.SeeChamo-nix.com** website. This gondola trip is expensive but can be a once-in-a-lifetime experience for many.

> **Tour Discounts for Geneva City Pass Holders:**
>
> Some tours to Chamonix and Mont-Blanc provide discounts to holders of the Geneva City Pass.

Try to get to the lower gondola sta-tion in central Chamonix early if possible. This is a popular des-tination and long-lines to get on the gondola are common. Also, be sure to wear warm clothes, even during hot summer days.

Traveling to Mont-Blanc: There are essentially three ways to travel to Chamonix from Geneva: car, bus, or group tour. Trains are not recommended due to the long amount of time required along with multiple train changes.

Car: Driving time is roughly an hour from central Geneva along pleasant highway. When arriving in Chamonix, there are several large parking lots just across the highway from the lower gon-dola station. One advantage of taking a car is that you can easily tack on a trip under the mountain into Italy.

Group Tour: Numerous firms provide full-day tours to Mont-Blanc. There are even private tour options. Check sites such as Viator.com or VisitACity.com (and others) for tour options.

Bus: Buses into Chamonix leave frequently and take up to 2-hours each way. One of the leading operators is **www.FlixBus.com**

Other Chamonix Attractions: Given the number of visitors to this mountain paradise, it is only natural for there to be many attractions in addition to the popular Mont-Blanc gondola. The Chamonix tourist office website is a great place to gain an overview of all that is available, En.Chamonix.com. Not all attractions are immediately in Chamonix, and some will require a short drive to nearby towns.

Some of the world-class offerings include:

- There are several cable cars leading to other mountain stops such as: Bellevue Cable Car, Brévant cable car, Flégère Gondola, and the lift up to Prarion ski area.

- The Montenvers-Mer de Glace train which provides a beautiful mountain ride to Montenvers, views of the Mer de Glacier, and to an ice cave in Montenvers.

- Tramway du Mont-Blanc – historic trains which depart for a mountain tour from Saint-Gervais-les-Bains, a village near Chamonix.

- Thermal spam the QC Terme spa on the edge of Chamonix.

- A ropes adventure park.

Enjoy your trip to Chamonix and Mont-Blanc, take time to capture some great memories, and then head back to beautiful Geneva.

The author hopes you have found this guide to the Geneva area beneficial.

~ ~ ~ ~ ~ ~

Starting-Point Travel Guides

www.StartingPointGuides.com

This guidebook on Geneva is one of several current and planned *Starting-Point Guides.* Each book in the series is developed with the concept of using one enjoyable city as your basecamp and then exploring from there.

Current guidebooks are for:

- Bordeaux, France and the surrounding Gironde River region.

- Dijon, France and the Burgundy Region.

- Gothenburg, Sweden and the Västra Götaland region.

- Lucerne, Switzerland and the Lake Lucerne area.

- Lyon, France and the Saône and Rhône confluence area.

- Nantes, France and the western Loire River valley.

- Strasbourg, France and the central Alsace region.

- Stuttgart, Germany and the Baden-Württemberg area.

- Toulouse, France and the Haute-Garonne district.

~ ~ ~ ~ ~

Updates on these and other titles may be found on the author's Facebook page at:

www.Facebook.com/BGPreston.author

Feel free to use this Facebook page to provide feedback and suggestions to the author or email to: cincy3@gmail.com

Made in the USA
Las Vegas, NV
27 April 2022

48072787R10075